Withdrawn Withdrawn

44785

MOHAWK SCHOOL
VANCOUVER
L

W9-BSM-458

ILLUSIONS ILLUSTRATED

ILLUSTRATED

A Professional Magic Show for Young Performers

JAMES W. BAKER

Drawings by JEANETTE SWOFFORD
Photographs by CARTER M. AYRES

Lerner Publications Company   Minneapolis

The photographers would like to thank the following children who appear in this book: Stephanie and Karen Leonard, Brent Smith, Kari Meyer, Joe Roling, Chris Hable, Kathy Graper, Jupy and Beta Femal, Mia, Danny, and Leah Lerner, Jennifer and Jeff Landt, and Leah Chatelle. Carter M. Ayres would also like to give special thanks to Mrs. Pat Leonard for her assistance in this project.

Copyright © 1984 by Lerner Publications Company

All rights reserved. International copyright secured.
No part of this book may be reproduced in any form whatsoever
without permission in writing from the publisher except for
the inclusion of brief quotations in an acknowledged review.

Manufactured in the United States of America

LIBRARY OF CONGRESS CATALOGING IN PUBLICATION DATA

Baker, James W., 1926-
  Illusions illustrated.

  Summary: A description of ten illusions, including
"Dollar in the Orange," "The Penetrating Ring," and "The
Thinking Cap," that together make up a complete magic
show with props, patter, and working. Concludes with a
ten-minute show of six tricks without props.
  1. Conjuring—Juvenile literature. 2. Tricks—Juvenile
literature. [1. Magic tricks] I. Swofford, Jeanette,
ill. III. Ayres, Carter M., ill. III. Title.
GV1548.B34 1984   793.8   83-19549
ISBN 0-8225-076814 (lib. bdg.)

1 2 3 4 5 6 7 8 9 10 92 91 90 89 88 87 86 85 84

*To my wife, Elaine—a nonmagician who, in
her own way, brought magic into my life—
for her love, her encouragement,
and her willingness, always, to "take a card, any card"*

Contents

Introduction   7

1 The World's
Greatest Magician   11

2 Dollar in the Orange   17

3 The Flying Scarf   25

4 Routined Ropes   31

   Cut and Restored Rope   31

   Spaghetti Factory   37

   Houdini Escape   43

   Two Ropes to One   47

5 Thinking Cap   51

6 The Penetrating Ring   57

7 The Flying Coin   63

8 An Impossible Prediction   69

9 Boxing a Ring   77

10 And, So, Good-Bye   83

11 Presentation, Patter,
and Miscellaneous Tidbits   87

12 A Ten-Minute Magic Show
without Props   97

   A Prediction   98

   Reading Your Thoughts   100

   Poor Handwriting   105

   A Miracle Prediction   108

   Predicting a Number   111

   The Disappearing Coin   115

   Conclusion   119

   About the Author   120

Introduction

Few people these days, other than professional stage magicians, can afford to spend a lot of time learning magic tricks. But many would enjoy being able to baffle and entertain their friends with a professional-caliber magic show, either in their homes or on the stages of their school auditoriums. It is for these people, who have a serious interest in performing real illusions but who have a minimum of time to devote to their preparation, that I have written *Illusions Illustrated*.

This book has evolved from over 20 years of experience performing, inventing, and experimenting with magic. As an amateur magician, I have performed before audiences in half a dozen countries. And I have read scores of books on magic. Over the years, I have come to realize that few books meet all of the special needs of nonprofessional magicians. *Illusions Illustrated* is different. I have been careful to include in this book only those illusions that can be performed successfully by any amateur. The illusions that I chose to write about have the following characteristics in common:

1. The illusions are meant to be performed, not just read. After all, performance is the end result of magic. There are many books filled with fascinating descriptions of how tricks are done—the secrets of illusions. They make delightful reading. But this is not that kind of book. The illusions presented here are meant to be performed.

2. The illusions meet the double test of being both baffling *and* entertaining. All of the illusions in this book have been audience-tested, and they have successfully fooled audiences as well as entertained them.

3. All of the illusions are equally effective before large and small audiences. There is no danger that an illusion performed on a stage before a large audience will be "lost." The tricks are just as impressive from far away as from close up.

4. The illusions can be learned with a minimum of tedious practice and without difficult sleight-of-hand moves. Notice that I didn't say "without practice." Some practice will be necessary to perform the illusions described here. But none requires endless hours of rehearsal or intricate hand manipulation.

5. The props, or special pieces of equipment needed to perform each illusion, are inexpensive and easy to find. Most props can be purchased from any magic shop. Many can be made from materials available around the house. In addition, all of the props are small and lightweight so that they can be transported easily to the place of the performance.

6. Each illusion can be performed without special stage arrangements. None of the effects in this book require trained assistants, special lighting, musical effects, or other elaborate setups that are often not available to the amateur magician.

To make learning these illusions as easy as possible, the effects are described in words, photographs, and sketches. The format for each illusion is the same.

First, under the heading EFFECT, the illusion is described as it is seen by the audience. Then, in a section called EQUIPMENT, the various props are described in detail. Next, under the heading WORKING, the operation of the illusion is described from the standpoint of the magician, making clear to the reader the difference between what the magician actually does and what the audience thinks he is doing. (Note: A magician may, of course, be either male or female. But because, as the author, I am describing the tricks as *I* do them, I will refer throughout to the magician as "he.") In the section called PATTER, a sample monologue, or line of patter, is presented. You are encouraged to read through the entire description—EFFECT, EQUIPMENT, WORKING, and PATTER—before practicing a trick.

Special emphasis has been given to patter, an aspect of magic that is too often ignored. Sometimes baffling effects fall flat because there is nothing to say during their performance, or because the patter that accompanies them is too unbelievable. The patter should complement the illusion, explain its reason for being, and enhance its entertainment value. But patter can only be suggested. Each person brings a unique personality to an effect. Although a complete patter line is included for each illusion presented here, you should not attempt to memorize it. Learn the thread of the story and use the words that come most naturally to you—words that fit your own personality.

And now for the first mystery of the evening. . . .

44785

MOHAWK SCHOOL
LEARNING CENTER
BENSENVILLE, IL

The World's Greatest Magician 1

EFFECT

The magician talks about the great magicians of history and then promises to show the audience a picture of the world's greatest magician. He displays a framed photograph, which turns out to be a picture of himself. Explaining that this is just a trick to show the audience an experiment involving the photograph, he turns the picture around so that the back of the frame faces the audience. Then he places the picture on a chair near the front of the stage, with the back side of the frame facing the audience.

The magician next hands out pencils and slips of paper and invites 15 or 20 people from the audience to write down the name of a famous person, living or dead. The slips are folded and dropped into a paper bag held by the magician. Then the magician returns to the stage, bringing a volunteer with him. He shakes up the folded slips in the bag and asks the volunteer to reach inside and select one at random. The slip is unfolded and read aloud.

The magician picks up the picture and shows it to the audience. Now his photograph is no longer in the frame! It has been mysteriously replaced by a photograph of the famous person whose name was on the slip of paper selected at random from the bag.

EQUIPMENT

For this magic trick, you will need an 8-by-10-inch framed photograph of a famous person—for example, Abraham Lincoln. In addition, you will have to make a *gimmick*, or trick picture, which is constructed as follows. Attach a photograph of yourself to the back of a separate piece of glass, which should be just large enough to fit over the glass in the picture frame. (This will be a little smaller than 8 by 10 inches.) Paste a section of newspaper to the back of your photograph. Take care to get a piece of newspaper containing text only—not photographs. You will need another folded newspaper, again a section without photographs, to place on your table during the actual performance.

You will also need a trick bag, called a *forcing bag.* This can easily be made from two identical paper bags, about lunch-bag size. Insert one bag inside the other and glue the two bags together on three pairs of sides, leaving the fourth pair of sides unglued. Separate the unglued sides of the two bags, forming an inner compartment. Into the inner bag place 15 or 20 folded slips of paper with the name "Abraham Lincoln" written on them in pencil. See FIGURES 1 and 2.

Finally, you will need a few pencils and blank slips of paper. Be sure that the slips

Fig. 1A   Fig. 1B

Fig. 1C   Fig. 1D

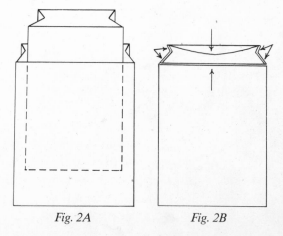

Fig. 2A   Fig. 2B

of paper are the same size, shape, and color as those that have already been folded and placed in the trick bag.

WORKING

All of the props described above are on your table. The gimmick with your picture is resting on top of the picture of Abraham Lincoln so that it looks as if your picture is in the frame. As you patter about great magicians through the ages, pick up the framed photograph with the gimmick on top.

Holding the gimmick on top with your fingers (thumb behind), show it to the audience, allowing plenty of time for everyone to see that it is a picture of you.

Fig. 2C

Lay the picture face down on top of the newspaper for just an instant while you use both hands to push up your sleeves. This is a natural misdirection move, which will not draw suspicion from the audience.

PATTER

There have been many great magicians throughout history ... Houdini, Mulholland, Blackstone, Thurston, Mark Wilson, and others. But do you know who is considered to be the greatest magician of all time? I've brought his picture along with me today so that I could show it to you. Here it is.

You might think that I'm a bit immodest, but, after all, I have to promote my own act! I can't afford an agent! Seriously, I brought this picture of myself along as a prop for an experiment I'd like to show you.

Once your sleeves are pushed up, pick up the picture again, this time leaving the gimmick behind on the newspaper.

Because the back of the gimmick is a piece of newspaper also, it is effectively camouflaged. Besides, the audience has its attention focused on the framed picture that you have just picked up, and not on anything on the table. Holding the picture (now the one of Abraham Lincoln) with its back to the audience, walk to the front of the stage and place it on a chair, back side to the audience. This must be a solid-backed chair, so that the volunteer you call later will not be able to see the picture until you are ready to present it.

Next, pass out pencils and blank slips of paper to 15 or 20 people in the audience. Invite them each to write down the name of a famous person, living or dead.

When they have done this, walk through the audience with the gimmicked paper bag, holding it so that anything dropped inside will fall into the outer bag between the two unglued sides.

Collect all of the slips and return to the stage, bringing a volunteer with you.

I'm going to leave my picture here on this chair in full view of all of you while we conduct a little experiment in mind reading.

As I pass out pencils and paper, I'd like you to think of some famous person. It can be any famous person—male or female, living or dead, American or other nationality. But he or she should be a famous person, one we are all likely to know. Write the name of your person on the slip of paper. After you have written down the name, fold the paper and drop it into this paper bag.

Now I'll need a volunteer to help me with the last part of the experiment. How about you?

Close the bag at the top and shake up the slips of paper inside.

When you open the bag, push the wall of the inner bag against the wall of the outer bag and grip the bag there. Then, when the volunteer reaches into the bag, he or she will have access only to the slips of paper that you had put there before the show—all of which bear the name of Abraham Lincoln.

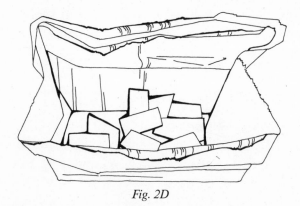

Fig. 2D

Have the volunteer read out the name on the slip of paper selected from the bag. It is Abraham Lincoln. Walk to the chair with the photograph on it.

Pick up the photograph of Abraham Lincoln and show it to the audience. It can be passed out for closer inspection.

Now I'll mix the names up in the bag and ask you to reach inside and select one.

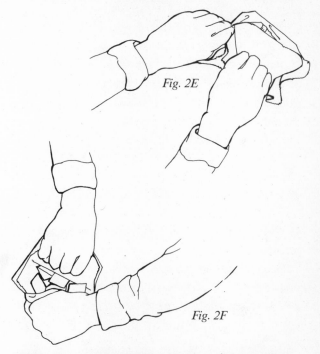

Fig. 2E

Fig. 2F

Will you read off the name, please? It's Abraham Lincoln? You'll remember that I placed a picture of myself on this chair. Let's take a look at it; you'll see why I placed it here. You thought that it was a picture of me.

Actually, it was a picture of Abraham Lincoln.

Dollar 2 in the Orange

EFFECT

The magician borrows a dollar bill from someone in the audience. The owner of the dollar bill writes down the serial number and signs his or her name on the bill for later identification. The bill is placed under a handkerchief and is given to another person in the audience to hold.

The magician then produces three oranges from a paper bag and sets them on a table. The dollar bill vanishes from under the handkerchief and appears inside one of the three oranges—the one selected by a volunteer from the audience.

EQUIPMENT

You will need a handkerchief, a piece of paper, a pen, three oranges, a large paper bag, and a sharp paring knife. Cut the piece of paper to the size of a dollar bill and roll it up. Then insert it into the hem of the handkerchief, as shown in the picture. When you start the trick, have the gimmicked handkerchief in your pocket. See FIGURE 3.

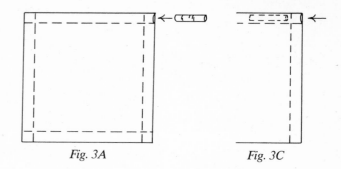

Fig. 3A   *Fig. 3C*

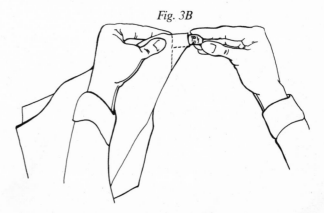

Fig. 3B

Prepare one of the three oranges by cutting a small hole in its bottom. Then push a large pencil or dowel (about ½ inch in diameter) up into the hole. Let the orange sit overnight in this manner, so that its juice dries up. The orange will have a neat little cylindrical hole inside when the pencil is removed the next day. The gimmicked orange is now ready. Place it, along with two normal oranges, into the paper bag for your performance. Have the sharp knife handy. See FIGURE 4.

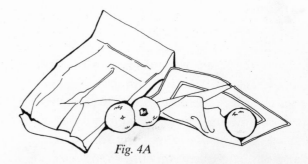

Fig. 4A

WORKING

Try to find someone in the audience who is willing to lend you a one-thousand-dollar bill. No one will, of course. You look dismayed.

Instead, borrow a one-dollar bill from someone in the audience. Before you take the bill back to the stage with you, ask the owner to write down the bill's serial number on a slip of blank paper.

In addition, have that person write his or her name on the bill and read the serial number out loud to the audience. The bill will now be unmistakably recognizable to all who see it.

Roll the bill into a small roll and, with your right hand, place the bill under your gimmicked handkerchief. As you do so, palm the dollar bill in your right hand.

In the same movement, pick up the rolled piece of paper in the hem of the handkerchief.

PATTER

I've heard it said that nobody trusts magicians; they're too sneaky. But I don't believe that's true. Today I want to test that theory and find out if you really can trust a magician. Will someone in the audience lend me a one-thousand-dollar bill?

I guess that proves you don't trust me. But maybe it's a matter of degree. Will someone trust me enough to lend me a one-dollar bill? Ah, there's a trusting person. Is this your dollar bill? How can you be sure? It doesn't have your name on it. We can remedy that. Here, take this pen and write your name on it. Also, write down the serial number on this slip of paper. Will you read out the serial number so the people in the audience can know it too? Anyone without a good memory can write it down.

There's something magical about this dollar bill—it comes from a trusting person. I'm going to roll it up and put it under my handkerchief to try to find out about its magical qualities.

Now, with your left hand, grasp the paper (which the audience thinks is the dollar bill) through the handkerchief, and call up a member of the audience to hold it for you. Make sure that a layer of handkerchief prevents the volunteer from seeing that the "dollar" is contained in the hem.

Now I'd like someone—anyone but the owner of the bill (that person might take it back)—to come up and hold onto it for me.

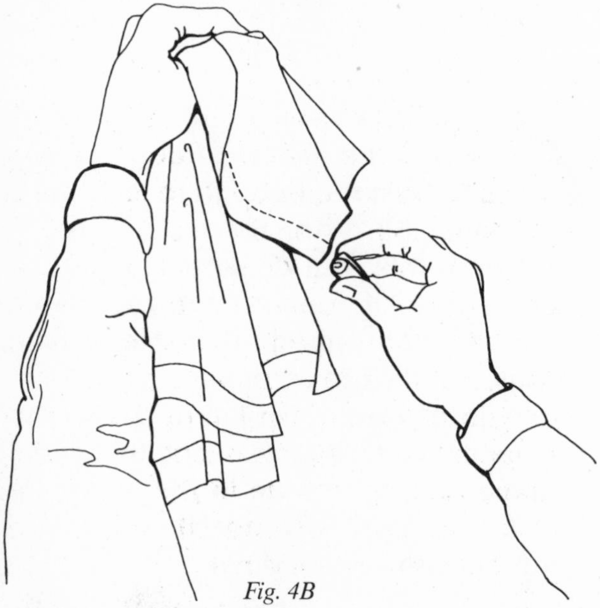

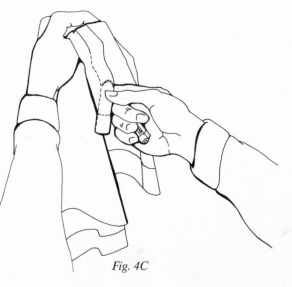

Fig. 4B

Fig. 4C

With the real dollar bill still palmed in your right hand, walk over to the paper bag on your table, 10 to 20 feet away from the volunteer. Reach inside to take out the oranges.

I want you to do a very difficult thing now. I want you to concentrate on the dollar bill you're holding with half of your mind, and on the three oranges over here with the other half of your mind.

When you reach inside the bag, push the rolled-up dollar bill into the hole in the bottom of the gimmicked orange.

With the same motion, take out that orange and place it on the table, bottom side down. In the same manner, reach into the bag again and take out the second orange, placing it next to the one on the table. Do the same for the third orange.

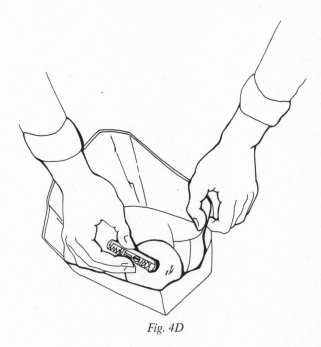

Fig. 4D

At this point you have almost completed the trick from your point of view, although it has hardly begun as far as the audience is concerned.

The person holding the fake dollar bill through the gimmicked handkerchief is still standing 10 to 20 feet away from the oranges on the table. Walk over to your volunteer and quickly grasp one corner of the handkerchief. Whisk the handkerchief out of his or her hand. The dollar bill has vanished.

Show the handkerchief all around, keeping one hand on the corner with the wadded paper. Put the handkerchief back in your pocket and take the volunteer over to the table.

Obviously, you were thinking about the oranges with *all* of your mind, and you forgot about the dollar bill. That's why it disappeared. And now let's see if you were really thinking about the oranges. If so, the dollar bill should be inside one of them.

Now you do a magician's *force* on the volunteer from the audience. It works like this: Ask the helper to select one of the three oranges. You know that the middle one contains the dollar bill. If the helper happens to select that one, fine.

You then slice into the orange through the sides, making sure you don't cut the dollar bill while doing so. When it is sliced, lift off the top half and have the volunteer take out the dollar bill. It will be slightly wet from the orange juice, lending a mysterious air to the trick.

If the helper points to one of the two oranges that do not contain the dollar bill, you will have to perform the magician's *force*.

Take the selected orange away and return it to the paper bag. If the helper selects the other orange without the dollar bill, repeat your previous actions. Put that orange into the bag as well.

This leaves one orange, the one containing the dollar bill. Proceed to slice it.

If, however, on the volunteer's second choice he or she selects the orange containing the dollar bill, simply pick that one up and set it aside, putting the other one back into the paper bag. This sounds simple, but it always gives the audience the impression that the volunteer freely selects the orange.

Now, I'd like you to tell me which orange is hiding the mysterious dollar bill. Select one, please.

Okay, we'll remove this one. Now select one of the two left.

Okay, we'll remove this one, too.

When the volunteer lifts the dollar bill from the orange, *do not* touch it yourself. Have the volunteer pull it out of the orange, open it up, read out the serial number to the audience, and return it to its owner. Then ask the owner to verify that it is the same dollar bill that he or she has just lent you a few minutes before.

Will you pull the bill out of the orange and read off the serial number, please? There is your dollar bill back. It proves that magicians are more than honest. The bill is in good shape. It has just a little orange juice on it. You can consider that as interest on your money.

The 3 Flying Scarf

EFFECT

The magician calls for two volunteers from the audience and asks them to stand facing each other, about 10 feet apart. He ties together two scarves, a red one and a blue one, and tucks them into the shirt collar of one of the volunteers. He then displays a multicolored scarf and places it in a box, which the other volunteer holds on top of his or her head.

The magician explains that he will cause the multicolored scarf to leave the box, go through the head of the volunteer, and fly out of the volunteer's mouth across the stage, whereupon the other volunteer is to catch it in his or her mouth.

Upon the count of three, nothing seems to happen. The magician tells the volunteers and the audience that the scarf actually flew so fast that no one could see it. He opens the box and shows that the multi-colored scarf has indeed left the box. Where is it?

The magician says that it flew through the air, into the other volunteer's mouth, and through that person's neck, and that it tied itself in between the red and blue scarves. Saying this, the magician whisks out the red and blue scarves from the other volunteer's shirt collar and shows that the multicolored scarf is there, tied between them.

EQUIPMENT

The props for this effect can be purchased at any magic shop or made at home. You will need a silky red scarf, a silky blue one, and two identical silky multicolored scarves which have at least one corner that is the same hue as the blue scarf. The scarves can be from 12 to 18 inches square; all should be the same size. The red scarf and one of the multicolored scarves need no special preparation.

Prepare the blue scarf and one of the multicolored scarves as shown in FIGURE 5. You will need to stitch a pocket into the folded blue scarf, so that the multicolored scarf that is tied to the blue scarf can be pulled inside the blue one almost all the way, with only the blue tip of the multicolored scarf sticking out. Thus prepared, the two scarves appear now to be simply a single blue one. These preparations should be made before you begin your performance.

The cardboard box, approximately 7 inches tall by 4½ inches wide, is the type in which popcorn is sometimes sold. It is prepared as shown in FIGURE 6. It is simply a box with an extra front glued onto it, forming a pocket into which a scarf can be shoved. With these two pieces of apparatus and some practice, you will be ready to perform the illusion.

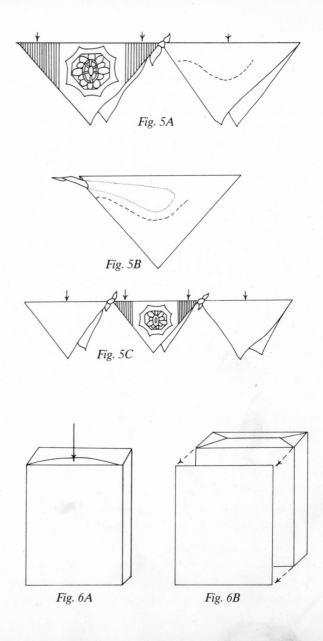

Fig. 5A

Fig. 5B

Fig. 5C

Fig. 6A

Fig. 6B

WORKING

Call two volunteers to the stage.

Place them about 10 feet apart, facing each other. Now tie the red and blue scarves together at the corners. Actually, you will tie the red scarf to the blue tip of the multicolored scarf protruding from inside the pocket in the blue scarf. The illusion is that you are tying the red and blue scarves together.

  Then tuck these scarves behind the shirt collar of one of the volunteers at the point where they are tied together, so that they hang out where the audience can see them.

Then place the unprepared multicolored scarf in the cardboard box. You actually shove it into the pocket formed by the additional front glued onto the box.

  Start to hand the box to the other volunteer. Instead, close the box and place it on the head of the other volunteer, asking that person to hold it there with both hands.

PATTER

I'd like to do an experiment that proves that silk scarves have an attraction for each other. It also proves that the scarf is quicker than the eye. Could I have two volunteers from the audience to assist me, please? Preferably two who cannot keep their mouths shut. All right, how about you? And you, over there?

Now if you'll just stand there quietly for a minute, I'll show you what I'm going to do. I'm going to tie this blue scarf to this red one. I'll need a place for safekeeping. This looks like a good place.

Now for a safe place for this scarf of many colors. It should be quite safe in here.

Tell the volunteers to keep their mouths open, because the scarf is going to fly from the box to the mouth of one of them, and then into the other's mouth. Speak first to the volunteer with the box on his or her head.

Then urge the other volunteer to keep his or her mouth open also.

If you're working with children, look out at the audience and say that it isn't necessary for them to keep their mouths open too.

Count to three.

Tap the cardboard box with your wand and ham it up as you pretend that the scarf flew across the stage.

Look disappointed when the audience does not see it.

I want both of you to open your mouths as wide as you can. I'm going to count to three, and then I'm going to tap the box with my magic wand. When I do, the scarf inside is going to jump through the box and inside your mouth. Then it's going to fly out of your mouth, across the stage, right to that person over there.

Now keep your mouth open and brace yourself, because that scarf will be coming very fast. When it flies to you, I want you to catch it in your teeth!

You there, in the front row, you don't have to keep your mouth open, too.

Okay, back to the flying scarf. Ready? Brace yourselves, because that scarf can fly very fast. One. Two. Three!

There it goes!

What? You didn't see it go? It certainly did. It just went so fast you couldn't see it. I'll show you.

Take the cardboard box from the volunteer's head and open it, holding the pocket closed with your thumb. Show the empty box to prove that the multicolored scarf has indeed vanished.

Walk across the stage to the other volunteer and whisk out from that person's collar the red and blue scarves, pulling them apart in the same motion. There, apparently tied between them, is the multicolored scarf that just vanished from the box.

Thank the two volunteers, ask the audience to give them a round of applause for their efforts, and send them back to their seats.

You see, it's not in the box. Where is it? It flew across the stage, into his (*her*) mouth, and right out the back of his (*her*) head.

And here it is, tied in between the two scarves we put there a minute ago, proving once and for all that the scarf is quicker than the eye.

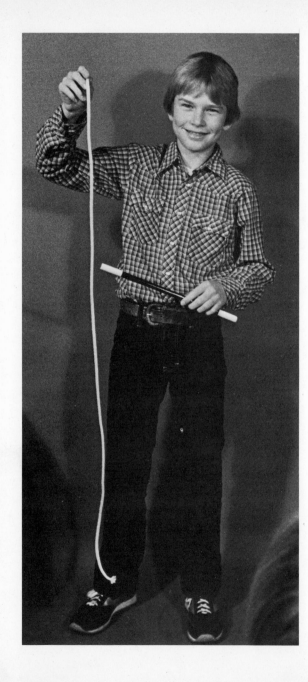

Routined Ropes 4

This chapter contains more than one illusion. It describes a routine that involves several separate illusions using only lengths of rope and a scissors. To the audience, this routine will appear as a series of related illusions, one leading into the other. For the sake of clarity, however, I will present the illusions separately, all within this chapter.

EFFECT

The magician shows a length of rope, cuts it in half, and then restores it to its original condition simply by sprinkling "woofle dust" over the cut.

Cut and Restored Rope

EQUIPMENT

This trick can be done with a piece of rope of any size from 3 to 6 feet. Because you will need the same piece for the next trick, though, make the rope for this effect exactly as described.

Obtain a piece of soft white cotton rope exactly 80 inches long—6 feet, 8 inches. (Magic shops sell special magician's rope, which is soft and pliable and is easily cut with scissors. This comes in 50- and 100-foot lengths and is well worth the investment for rope tricks.) You will also need a strong, heavy scissors.

Mark the rope at certain points along its length. This can be done with a pencil; better still, the rope can be wrapped at these points with "invisible" cellophane tape. Wrap the first piece of tape around one end of the rope. Wrap the second piece at a point 8 inches from the end. Wrap the third piece at a point 12 inches from the last piece of tape. Wrap the fourth piece at a point 24 inches from the last one. Wrap the fifth piece at the other end of the rope, which is 36 inches from the last piece. The clear tape will not be seen by the audience. See FIGURE 7.

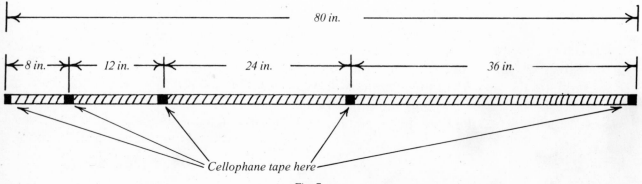

Fig. 7

WORKING

PATTER

Scouts are always working with ropes. They tie square knots, round knots . . . even knew one that could tie an oblong knot. They tie sheepshanks, goat shanks, and donkey shanks. I heard of one scout who tied up the scout leader by the shanks. I can do a few tricks with ropes, but I didn't learn them in the Scouts!

I learned how to perform this little miracle on a woofle dust farm. That's where they grow woofle dust plants to make woofle dust for magicians. All magicians use it to make their magic work. Look, I'll show you some.

Reach into your pocket and take out some imaginary woofle dust and sprinkle it in the air.

Couldn't you see it? Of course not. Woofle dust is invisible. How could it be magical if it weren't invisible? I'll show you how this woofle dust can do something magical to this piece of rope.

Stretch the 80-inch length of rope between your hands, giving it several hard jerks to show that it is solid.

Bring the two ends together in your left hand and hold them between your fingers and thumb so that the two ends stick up about four inches, and the rest of the rope loops down below.

Reach down and pick up the center of the rope with your right hand. Bring it up, behind your left hand (from the audience's point of view). Your right thumb and forefinger should be sticking through the loop.

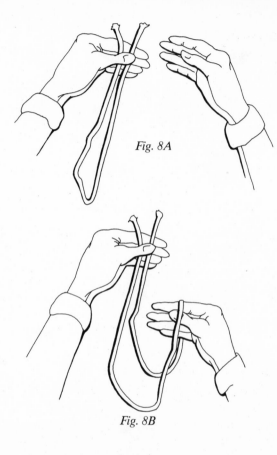

Fig. 8A

Fig. 8B

When your right hand is behind your left hand, your right thumb and forefinger catch hold of the piece of rope to the left in your left hand and pull that through the loop and up, so that a small loop now sticks up above your hand.

Next, cut the rope at the loop that is sticking up, right through the first piece of cellophane tape, letting the two long loose ends fall down. You have not cut the rope in the center, though it appears to the audience that you have. You have actually cut it at a point 8 inches from one end.

Now I'll cut the rope at the middle and tie it back together.

Next, tie the two short ends of the rope together. Actually, you are tying the 8-inch length around the longer length of rope. To the audience it looks as though you have just cut a long length of rope in half and tied the two halves together.

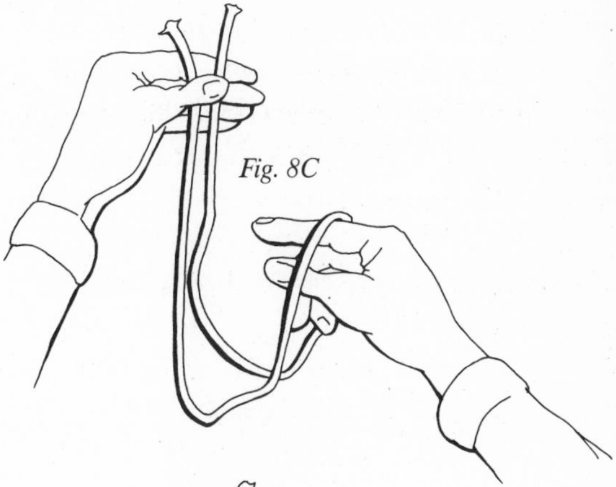

Fig. 8C

To restore the cut rope, stretch it out to its full length and wind the entire length around your left hand with your right hand.

As you wind, the knot will eventually come into your right hand. When it does, take the knot, concealing it in your right hand, and slide it down the rope as you wind.

When your right hand finishes winding, you will have slid the knot off the end. Hold it in your right hand.

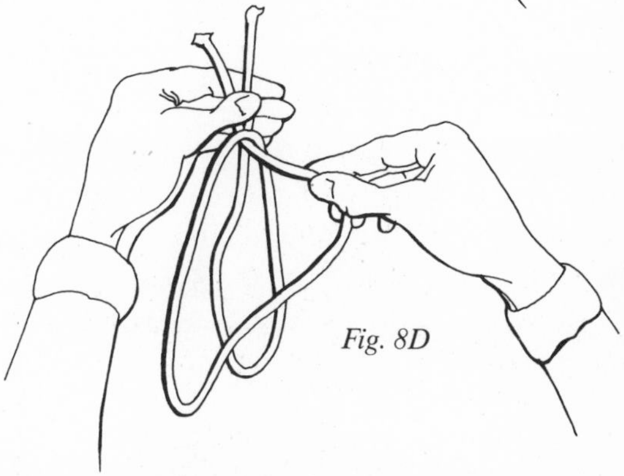

Fig. 8D

To get rid of it, immediately reach into your right pocket to get out the imaginary "woofle dust" to restore the rope. Leave the knot in your pocket.

Sprinkle the "woofle dust" over your left hand, which contains the coiled rope. Then unwind the rope and show the audience that it has been restored to its original length.

Now here's where the woofle dust comes in handy. I'll sprinkle some on the rope, and . . .

Although the rope now is actually 8 inches shorter than it originally was, this small amount will not be noticed by the people in the audience. To them, you cut the rope in the middle and restored it to its full length.

The drawings in FIGURE 8 show how the rope is manipulated.

You'll see that the woofle dust has magically restored it.

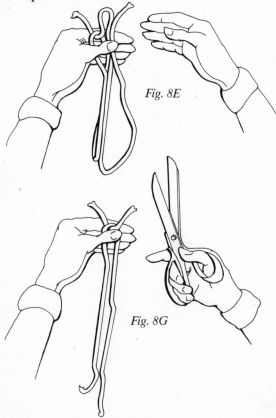

Fig. 8E

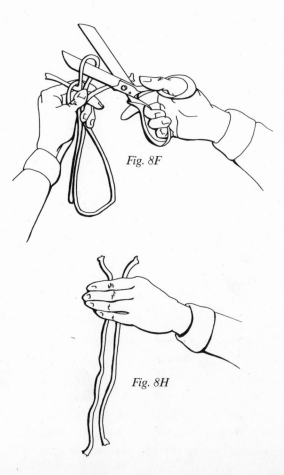

Fig. 8F

Fig. 8G

Fig. 8H

EFFECT

Move immediately into this illusion from the cut-and-restored rope trick. Having cut away the first 8 inches of the 80-inch length of rope, you now have in your hand a length of rope 72 inches long, marked off with cellophane tape into lengths of 12, 24, and 36 inches.

The audience then sees you cut this 72-inch length of rope into three pieces unequal in length: one 12-inch piece, one 24-inch piece, and one 36-inch piece. These you refer to as "a short piece," "a middle-sized piece," and "a long piece."

Then the audience sees you stretch the three pieces of rope, making them all the same length, and once again turn them back into three unequal pieces.

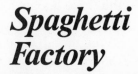

Spaghetti Factory

EQUIPMENT

All you need is the 72-inch length of rope, which is cellophane-taped as described above, and a scissors.

WORKING

Stretch out and show the 72-inch length of rope.

Cut the 72-inch piece of rope (at the points marked by the cellophane tape) into three unequal lengths—one 12-inch, one 24-inch, and one 36-inch piece.

Hold the three unequal lengths of rope in your left hand between the fingers (to the front) and the thumb (to the rear), about 6 inches from the ends.

PATTER

I've had a lot of jobs in my time. I told you I once worked on a woofle dust farm. The woofle dust market dried up and I got another job—working in a spaghetti factory. This was a very specific assembly-line job. When a long piece of spaghetti came by on a conveyor belt, I had to cut it up into pieces of equal length. I'll show you what I mean with this piece of rope. My boss warned me that if I wanted to keep my job I had to cut all the pieces of spaghetti the same length. I did very well for a while. But one night I was working late and I got very sleepy. Before I knew it, I had goofed up. I had cut the spaghetti in the wrong places, like this.

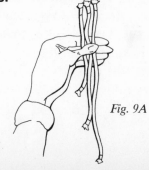

Fig. 9A

The top ends of the three pieces of rope are together, with the bottom ends hanging down at unequal distances. The ropes are arranged in your left hand from left to right (from your own point of view), the short one, the middle-sized one, and the long one.

Reach down with your right hand and take the bottom end of the long rope. Bring it up and place it in your left hand alongside (and to the right of) the other three ends.

    Reach down and take the bottom end of the middle-sized rope. Bring it up behind the loop of the long rope and place it in your left hand alongside (and to the right of) the end of the long rope.

Pay special attention to the next move. There now should be five ends of rope in your left hand.

    With your right thumb and forefinger, reach over the first two pieces of rope and under the second two pieces and grip the short piece of rope by its bottom end. Pull it up over the left thumb and place it in the left hand to the far left of the five ends of rope already there. Grip this one also with your left thumb.

    You now have six ends of rope sticking up from your left hand, and three loops hanging down.

When I looked at the three pieces of spaghetti, I knew I had made a mistake. Then I knew I was in even more trouble because I heard my boss's footsteps coming down the hallway. As they got nearer and nearer, I folded up the three pieces of spaghetti like this.

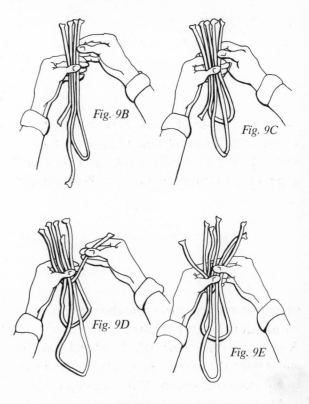

Fig. 9B

Fig. 9C

Fig. 9D

Fig. 9E

With your right hand, grasp the three ends to the right, and with your left hand, grasp the three ends to the left. Pull your hands apart and the ropes will stretch into what appear to be three pieces, all of equal length (24 inches long).

Just then the door opened, and the boss walked in. "Are you cutting all those pieces of spaghetti the same length?" he asked. "Yes sir," I answered.

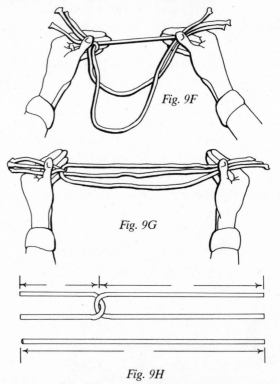

Fig. 9F

Fig. 9G

Fig. 9H

What actually has happened is shown in FIGURE 9H. The left hand hides from the audience the point where the short (12-inch) rope is looped through the long (36-inch) rope.

Now you are ready to show the audience the three equal lengths of rope, one at a time. Reach over with your right hand and take the middle-sized rope at a point about 6 inches down from the top and bring it away to the right in your right hand, counting as you do so.

I said, "I'm cutting them all the same length, just as you told me to. . . . You see. . . ."

"One."

Bring the rope in your right hand back to your left hand, secretly substituting it for the two linked ropes. Bring the two linked ropes away to the right in your right hand (leaving the single, middle-sized rope in your left hand), counting as you do so.

While holding the two looped ropes in your right hand, reach over and take the middle-sized rope from your left hand.

Remember, always hold the two looped ropes at the point where they loop together so that the audience will not see that they are looped together.

Next, forcefully throw all the ropes on the floor and pick them up one at a time, showing that they have returned to their original states.

The moves for the Spaghetti Factory trick are shown in the series of drawings in FIGURE 9.

"Two."

"Three."

The boss was so happy that he gave me a raise and left the room smiling. But after he left, I thought about how crazy the whole thing was. Why do pieces of spaghetti have to be the same length? You eat them all anyway. So I threw the three pieces on the floor, and when I picked them up there was a short piece, a middle-sized piece, and a long piece.

EFFECT

The magician shows two lengths of rope, each about 8 or 9 feet long. He patters about Houdini, the great magician, and his ability to escape from anything. The magician takes off his jacket or sweater and threads the two ropes through the sleeves. He puts his jacket back on as an improvised straightjacket. His arms are then tied across his front in a crisscross fashion.

When the magician is thus bound, two volunteers from the audience come up and tightly hold the ends of the rope. The magician patters about how Houdini never revealed the secret of how he escaped from a straightjacket like this one. With that, the magician escapes before the eyes of the audience, while the two volunteers are still holding the ends of the rope.

Houdini Escape

EQUIPMENT

You will need two pieces of rope about 8 or 9 feet long, equal in length, and a short piece of white thread. Lay the two pieces of rope side by side and tightly tie them together with the piece of white thread in the exact center. Then double the two ropes back as shown in FIGURE 10.

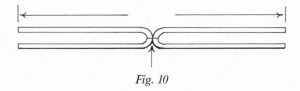

Fig. 10

WORKING

Have the two ropes on your table. Pick them up, holding them at the point where they are tied together with the white thread. Show them to the audience.

PATTER

One of the greatest magicians of all time was Houdini. He was famous for many great illusions, but he was known primarily for his wonderful escapes. He could escape from anything—jails, locks, handcuffs, sealed and nailed boxes. Anything. Once he even escaped from a straight jacket. This was his most famous escape. Many of Houdini's secrets have been revealed in books written by his assistants, but the straight jacket escape was his most closely guarded secret. He never told anyone how he did it. In fact, Houdini took that secret with him to the grave.

Take off your jacket or sweater and, working from its inside, thread two ends of the rope through the right sleeve so the two ends hang out the bottom of the sleeve about 3 feet.

Thread the other two ends through the left sleeve so the ends hang out the bottom of that sleeve about 3 feet also.

In doing this, adjust the ropes so that the point where they are tied with the white thread goes slightly into one sleeve and cannot be seen by the audience.

With the jacket or sweater thus prepared, hold it up for the audience to see, and then put it on as you usually do. Two ends of rope will be hanging out of each sleeve. Call for two volunteers from the audience.

Give the two rope ends hanging from the left sleeve to the volunteer on your left, making sure that the person faces the audience.

Give the two rope ends hanging from the right sleeve to the volunteer on your right, making sure that this person also faces the audience.

Ask each volunteer to give you *one* of the ends he or she is holding.

Take one end of rope from each volunteer; tie these together in a simple knot, pull it up

I certainly don't know how he did it. No one does. But I'd like to give you an idea of what an incredible mystery this was. I'll improvise a straight jacket with my jacket (*sweater*) and these two pieces of rope. Houdini's straight jacket looked something like this.

Now, if I can have a couple of volunteers from the audience, I'll show you how Houdini would have tied himself up.

Would you please hold these two ends of the ropes?

And would you please hold the other two ends?

Would you both please give me one of the rope ends you're holding?

Now, the arms of the straight jacket were crossed in front, like this.

snug, crossing your arms as you do so, and
hand the opposite ends back to the volunteers.
They are now each holding two ends of the
rope again.

Ask them to pull hard on the ropes. When
they do, the thread breaks silently and
you can walk away from the ropes. Each
volunteer is still holding two ends of rope.

**Now, each of you hold tightly to your
ends of the ropes. And this will give you
an idea of the impossibility of escape
that Houdini faced. Now please pull
tightly on the ropes.**

**I'm sorry that I can't explain this miraculous escape for you today, but, as I said
before, Houdini never revealed the secret of this great mystery.**

EFFECT

The magician shows the audience two short lengths of rope. In a flash they melt into one single rope twice as long. Then the magician ties a knot in the longer piece of rope, and, in a flash, two more knots appear.

EQUIPMENT

You will need three pieces of rope: one piece 30 inches long and two pieces each 14 inches long. Tie a tight overhand knot at each end of the longer (30-inch) length of rope. Tie a tight overhand knot at one end only of each of the two shorter (14-inch) pieces of rope. Attach the unknotted ends of the short ropes to the longer rope by looping the ends around the longer rope and tying or sewing them with white thread. See FIGURE 11.

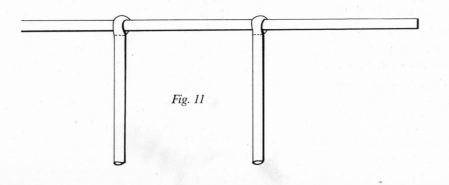

Fig. 11

Two Ropes
to One

WORKING

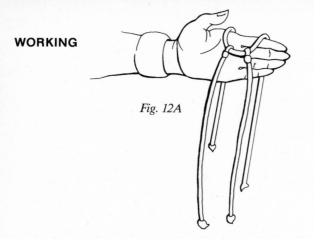

Fig. 12A

Slide the two short pieces of rope to a point near the center of the longer rope. They should be about 1½ inches apart.

Drape the ropes over your left hand so that the two short pieces fall behind your left hand and the ends of the longer rope hang down in front of your left hand (from the audience's point of view).

The audience will think that you are holding two short but separate lengths of rope. (See FIGURE 12 for the magician's view and the audience's view.) With your right hand, grasp the short rope on the right where it loops around the longer rope. Use your left hand at the same time to grasp the corresponding point on the other short rope.

PATTER

Have you ever heard anyone say that the hand is quicker than the eye? Today I'm going to prove that the hand is quicker than the mouth. I'll use my hands and your mouths.

I have two short pieces of rope.

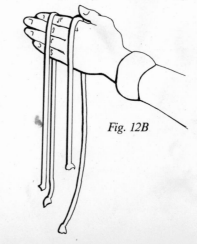

Fig. 12B

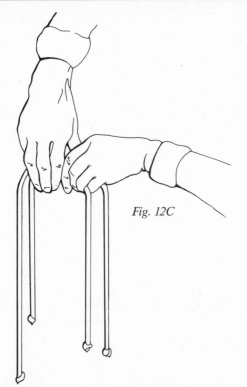

Fig. 12C

I'm going to turn these two into one piece of rope quicker than you can say the magic words, *irribatti wambadoo,* thus proving the hand is quicker than the mouth. All right. I'll count to three, and when I do you say, "Irribatti wambadoo." One. Two. Three.

As you reach the count of three, pull your hands apart, sliding the loops along the longer rope until they stop at the knots in the end of the longer rope. Your hands cover the loops and knots, and make it appear that you are now holding one long length of rope. The audience has finished saying the magic words.

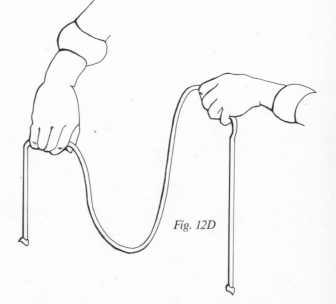

Fig. 12D

What took you so long? I've been waiting for you. I told you the hand was quicker than the mouth. Now I'm going to tie a single knot in this rope.

The backs of your hands are facing the audience. Work your hands around so that the backs of your hands are facing away from the audience, but at the same time continue to conceal the knots in your clenched fists.

Thus holding and covering the knots, make a large, loose overhand knot in the rope.

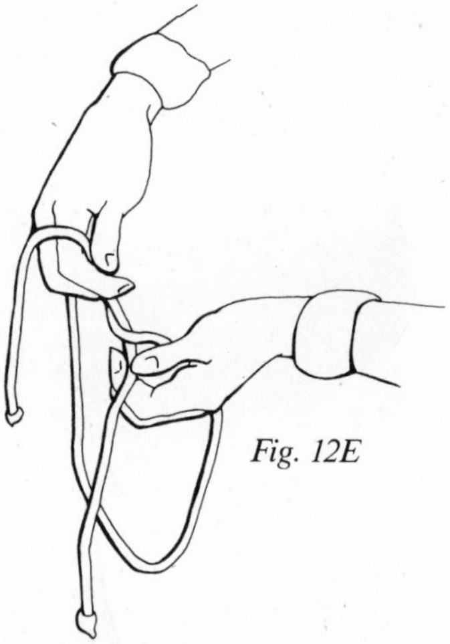

Fig. 12E

And now I'm going to tie two more knots in it before you can say the magic words. Again, on the count of three. One. Two. . . . Three!

As you reach the count of three, pull hard on the ropes, thus tightening the knot in the middle and revealing the two knots which had been covered by your hands. Suddenly the rope has three knots along its length.

There are the three knots in the rope. And I've proved that, indeed, the hand is quicker than the mouth.

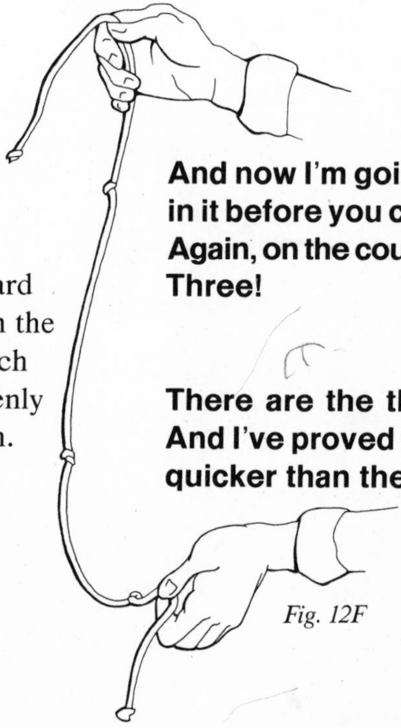

Fig. 12F

Thinking Cap 5

EFFECT

The magician calls up a volunteer and has that person select a card at random from a deck. The volunteer looks at the card and then puts it into his or her pocket, showing it to no one. The remainder of the deck is put away.

The magician asks the volunteer to concentrate on the selected card and to try to project his or her thoughts to the members of the audience. The magician says that people in the audience who get a clear picture of the chosen card should raise their hands. No one does.

Then the magician puts a "thinking cap" on the volunteer. Unknown to the volunteer, the thinking cap has a card stuck to the front of it. Now, when the magician asks if anyone in the audience gets a clear mental picture of the chosen card, almost everyone raises his or her hand and calls out the name of the card, to the surprise of the volunteer, who confirms that the audience has identified the chosen card.

The magician removes the thinking cap from the volunteer's head and the volunteer returns to the audience, wondering how everyone knew the selected card. The people in the audience know, of course, but they still cannot figure out how the magician knew which card the volunteer would select.

EQUIPMENT

This is an amusing variation on an old magical effect involving the "forcing" of a card. There are dozens of ways to force a card, many of them requiring extensive sleight of hand. Perhaps the simplest and most fool-proof method for the beginner is the use of a Svengali deck of cards. These decks are well known to all magicians but not to many lay-men. They are available at magic shops and are not expensive.

A Svengali deck consists of 52 cards—26 cards that are assorted and 26 that are exactly alike. The latter group might contain 26 tens of hearts, for example. And all of the identical cards are slightly shorter than the assorted cards. Thus when the pack is flipped one way the viewer sees only the assorted cards because the identical cards are behind the assorted cards. When the pack is flipped the other way the viewer sees only the identical cards—in this example, the tens of hearts.

Thus the magician can riffle the cards before the volunteer, having the volunteer stick a finger in the deck at any point. The volunteer will always select the ten of hearts no matter where he or she inserts a finger in the pack.

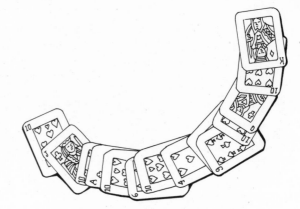

Fig. 13

For this trick, you will also need an old hat. This can be a party hat purchased from a variety store, or any old hat—the funnier-looking, the better. I use an old turban. See FIGURE 13 for pictures of these props.

WORKING

Call up a volunteer.

Flip the cards, letting the volunteer see that they are all different, although you don't say this. There is no reason to suggest that the deck is anything but an ordinary one.

PATTER

I'd like to try a little experiment in thought transference, or what is commonly called *mind reading.* This will be something different from the usual mind reading act, however. Today, I'm going to prove that anyone can be a mind reader. In fact, I'm going to show that you people here have the ability to read other people's thoughts. But we'll have to have someone whose thoughts you can read. Would someone volunteer to come up and help with this experiment?

I hope you have great powers of concentration, because this experiment requires them. First, I want you to select a card at random from this pack.

Then turn the deck over, so that the volunteer can see only the backs of the cards.

I am going to flip through this deck of cards, like this, and I'd like for you to insert your finger in the deck at any point that suits your fancy.

The volunteer inserts a finger in the deck.

There, take that card. Please take it carefully so I can't see which card it is.

The volunteer picks out the card, looks at it, and places it in his or her pocket.

You look at it, but don't show it to anyone. Remember the card and then put it in your pocket.

Put the remainder of the deck on the table.

Now I'd like for you to concentrate on that card. Think of nothing else. Put all other thoughts out of your mind. I'd also like for there to be absolute quiet in the room so we have every chance of transferring this person's thoughts to the people in the audience. Now, if anyone gets a clear mental picture of the card this volunteer chose and is thinking about, please raise your hand. Remember, don't guess. Only raise your hand if you have a clear mental picture.

No one gets a clear mental picture and no one raises a hand. Try this several times.

Are you sure you're concentrating on your card? I don't think you're thinking

Prior to the performance you have cellophane-taped the force card (for example, the ten of hearts) to the front of the old hat. The hat is sitting on the table, facing the rear so that the card taped to the front of it cannot be seen.

Pick up the hat, covering the card on the front of it with your hands, and quickly put it on the volunteer's head. Make sure that this is a natural movement; pick up the hat with two hands, one at each end of the hat.

Also, make sure the volunteer doesn't see the card, which is now visible to the audience.

Members of the audience will begin raising their hands as they see the ten of hearts clearly before them on the thinking cap.

After several people have named the ten of hearts, turn to the volunteer.

The volunteer returns the card to you, saying it was indeed the ten of hearts.

Set the thinking cap on the table with the card facing to the rear. Conceal the card with your hand as you remove it.

hard enough. That's the problem. I believe you need the help of a thinking cap.

Once again I'd like for you to think of the card you chose, putting all other thoughts out of your mind. And if anyone in the audience gets a clear mental picture of the card, please raise your hand.

It looks as if the cap is helping. What mental picture do you get? And you?

What card did you select? May I see?

Thank you very much for helping me prove that mind reading can be easy if you will only use your powers of concentration—and a little help from a thinking cap.

The Penetrating Ring

6

57

EFFECT

The magician borrows a finger ring from someone in the audience. After placing it under a scarf, he calls forth a volunteer to hold the ring through the cloth.

The magician next summons two more volunteers. While holding a magic wand at the center, he asks each volunteer to hold an end of the wand in a tight grip. The magician then takes the ring—still under the cloth—from the first volunteer, and places it against the back of the hand that is gripping the wand.

With a mighty push, the magician shoves the ring through the back of his hand. Releasing the wand, he reveals that the ring is encircled on the wand, although both volunteers are still tightly gripping the two ends of the wand.

EQUIPMENT

You will need a large, square colorful head scarf with a fairly wide hem. Into the hem in one corner of the scarf sew a cheap ring; a small curtain ring will work nicely. Most women's scarves have a small label sewn into one corner. It is a good idea to sew the ring inside the hem in that corner, so you will have an easy way to identify the corner of the scarf containing the ring.

The other piece of equipment necessary is a magic wand. This should be a thin one, approximately ¼ inch in diameter, of the type that comes with children's magic sets. If you don't have one, use a 12- or 14-inch dowel painted black with white tips. See FIGURE 14.

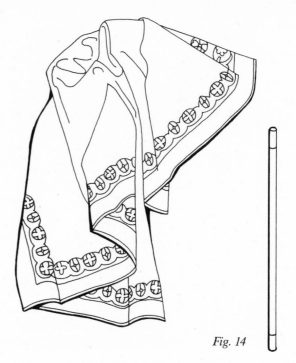

Fig. 14

PATTER

Every magician likes to feel trusted by the audience. And it's common for magicians to borrow things. Many ask to borrow 50-cent pieces. Others ask to borrow dollar bills. I'm not going to ask for anything like that. All I'd like to borrow is a very valuable ring. Something sentimental . . . and, of course, expensive.

WORKING

Borrow a ring from someone in the audience, taking care to select a thin, fairly plain one that will feel like the one sewn into the corner of the scarf. Show the ring to everyone.

Place the ring under the scarf with your right hand. Hold the scarf so that the corner containing the sewn-in ring is toward the back, that is, away from the view of the audience.

As you bring the real ring down behind the scarf and begin to move it under the scarf, slip it into the palm of your hand and hold it there with your fingers. At the same time, catch the sewn-in ring with your thumb and forefinger. See FIGURE 15.

There is no need to worry about any difficult palming; your hand is out of sight under the scarf, anyway. This move must be smooth and continuous, without hesitation, so as not to give any indication of a switch of rings.

Once your hand is under the scarf, the sewn-in ring is pushed up to the center of the scarf and is gripped from the top, through the scarf, with your left hand. Call up the first volunteer.

Oh, fine. There's someone who trusts the magician.

I'm glad to see someone trusts me with a finger ring. Most people won't even trust me with the ring in the bathtub! I can look at this ring and tell not only that it is valuable, but also that it is shy. Therefore, I'm going to put it under this scarf so that it will have a private place to change—into, perhaps, a thousand-dollar bill.

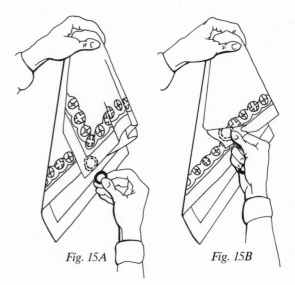

Fig. 15A   *Fig. 15B*

Now, will someone please come up and hold this ring for safekeeping?

Give the ring to the first volunteer with your left hand, making sure that person gets a tight grip on it.

Straighten the volunteer's arm so that he or she is less likely to look under the scarf. The borrowed ring is now in your right hand.

Walk over to your table and pick up your magic wand, holding it with one end in each hand. While talking, slip the borrowed ring (in your right hand) onto the end of the wand and slide it, inside your fist, to the center of the wand. See FIGURE 16.

Having called two more volunteers, ask them to hold tightly to the ends of the wand.

Ask the first volunteer to hand you the ring (under the scarf).

Take the ring in your left hand. At this point you might try to trick the two volunteers holding the wand into releasing their grips. They won't fall for it.

That's right, hold it there, tightly, now; get a good grip on it and don't drop it. Hold it right there where everyone can see it.

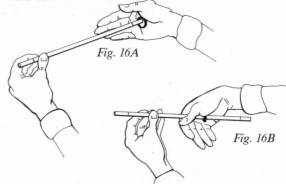

Fig. 16A

Fig. 16B

Now, I'd like to get two more people to assist me. You hold this end of the magic wand. And you, hold the other end. Get a good, tight grip, and please don't let me trick you into letting go of the wand.

Now, please hand me the ring back.

Take the ring and press it and the scarf, together, against the back of your hand.

Gripping the scarf at some other point, count to three, and, on three, snatch the scarf away and release your grip on the wand and ring with your right hand. Give the ring a spin as you do so.

Walk away, leaving the two volunteers still holding the ends of the wand with the ring spinning on the middle of the wand.

Okay, if I can't slip the ring on the wand from either end, there's only one route left. That's through the hand and onto the middle of the wand.

One . . . two . . . three!

And there, my friend, is your valuable ring . . . not a mere thousand-dollar bill.

The 7 Flying Coin

EFFECT

The magician borrows a penny or dime from a volunteer in the audience and has that person note its date and mark it by scratching the coin. He then places it under a handkerchief and has the volunteer hold the coin through the handkerchief.

The magician removes from his pocket a small box encircled with rubber bands and asks a second volunteer from the audience to hold the box on his or her palm.

When the magician whisks the handkerchief away from the hand of the first volunteer, he reveals that the coin has disappeared. The second volunteer opens the rubber-banded box, finding inside a second box (a match box), also encircled with rubber bands. Inside this is a third box bound up with rubber bands. And inside this box is a tiny cloth bag whose neck is closed with a rubber band. Inside the bag is the same coin, which can be identified by the date and the scratch marks.

EQUIPMENT

All of the equipment needed for this trick can be made with materials found around the house.

You will need a small wooden box approximately 3 inches long, 2 inches wide, and 1 inch high, the top of which is hinged on with adhesive tape; an ordinary match box with a sliding drawer; and a little cloth bag 1 inch long by ¾ inch wide.

You will also need 9 rubber bands and a gimmick. This gimmick is a metal chute 3 inches long, ¾ inch wide, and just thick enough to allow a penny or a dime to slide through it easily. It can be cut from a metal curtain rod, smoothed at the ends, and bent to allow the coin to slide through it easily.

In addition, you will need a handkerchief with a wide border into which is sewn a penny or dime at one corner. See FIGURE 17.

To prepare for performing the trick, place the handkerchief in a convenient pocket with the "coin corner" in a position where you can readily take hold of it.

The boxes are prepared like this: Place one end of the chute into the neck of the little bag and encircle it with a rubber band. Then place the bag, with the chute sticking out, into the match box, again with the chute sticking out, and encircle the match box with

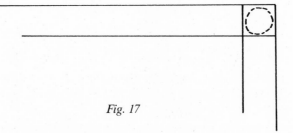

Fig. 17

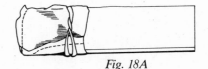

Fig. 18A

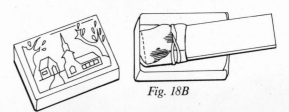

Fig. 18B

four rubber bands. Place the nested boxes, again, with the chute sticking out, into the largest box, and encircle that one with four rubber bands. See FIGURE 18.

The entire batch of boxes is placed in your right front pocket with the chute pointing upward. (Be sure to wear pants or a skirt with roomy pockets!)

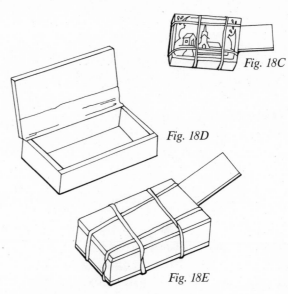

Fig. 18C

Fig. 18D

Fig. 18E

WORKING

Have the prepared box in your right pocket and the prepared handkerchief in your left pocket.

Try to borrow some money from people in the audience.

No one agrees to lend you a thousand-dollar bill. You act surprised.

PATTER

A few minutes ago that person over there showed trust by letting me borrow a ring. You did get your ring back, didn't you? Now that I've proven I'm trustworthy, I'd like to borrow some money. Is there anyone in the audience who'd be willing to lend me . . . a thousand-dollar bill?

People volunteer to lend you a penny.

Walk over to one of the people offering to lend you a penny and take the coin. At the same time lead that person back to the stage with you.

Have the volunteer scratch the coin with an identifying mark so that it can be recognized later, and note the date of the coin.

Take out your prepared handkerchief.

Slowly place the coin under the handkerchief, letting the audience see the coin go under the handkerchief.

Just as the coin goes out of sight under the handkerchief, palm it and take the coin that is sewn into the corner of the hem between your thumb and forefinger. Push this coin up

How about a penny? Is there anyone here who would lend me a penny?

I guess that demonstrates how much people trust a magician.

Here is a person who trusts a magician— to some extent, anyway. But I don't want you to trust me too far with your money. Why don't you come along with me? You don't want to get too far away from your hard cash.

Are you sure this is your money? It doesn't have your name on it. Maybe you'd better put your name on it, or at least a mark, so you'll know it's the same coin the next time you see it. And make a note of the penny's date.

I'm going to place your penny under my handkerchief and ask you to hang on to it for safekeeping.

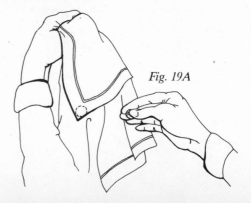

Fig. 19A

under the handkerchief to the center of the handkerchief. See FIGURE 19.

Ask the volunteer to grasp his or her coin through the handkerchief. Actually, the volunteer holds the coin previously sewn into the corner of the hem.

Withdrawing your hand from under the handkerchief (it contains the marked coin), immediately reach into your right pocket. When your hand is inside your pocket, drop the marked coin into the chute. The coin slides into the bag in the series of boxes.

Immediately withdraw the chute from the boxes and leave it in your pocket. Bring out the box wrapped in rubber bands.

Call for another volunteer, and ask that person to hold the box on the palm of his or her hand. Have this person stand across the stage about 10 feet from the first volunteer, who is still holding a coin under the handkerchief.

Walk back over to the first volunteer, explaining that the coin will fly across the room to the box.

There you are. Get a good grip on it so that it doesn't get away, and hold it in front of you so that everyone can see.

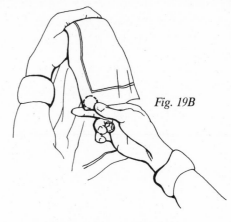

Fig. 19B

Now I'd like another volunteer to come up and hold this box for me.

Do you have very sensitive fingers? If you do, you'll feel the coin getting thinner and thinner. Soon it's going to get so thin it'll float out from under the handkerchief, fly across the room, and find its way inside the box that volunteer is holding. Can you feel it getting thinner and thinner?

No matter what the first volunteer says, reach up and take the handkerchief by the corner and whisk it away. The coin has disappeared.

Remain near the first volunteer, and ask the second one to open the box he or she holds.

Now, will you please open the box you're holding?

As that volunteer opens each successive box and finally the bag, you ask him or her to hold them up and tell the audience what he or she is doing.

Finally, the second volunteer discovers the marked coin inside the little cloth bag. You send the first volunteer over to identify it.

Now would you go over and identify your penny? Is it yours? It may not have your name on it, but it does have your mark—the one you scratched there a moment ago.

The coin has mysteriously disappeared from under the handkerchief and reappeared magically inside a small bag that was inside a series of three banded boxes.

Thank your volunteers for their assistance.

I want to thank you very much for helping me prove that you can trust a magician—at least with a penny. How about a round of applause for my two assistants?

An Impossible 8 Prediction

EFFECT

The magician selects five people in the audience at random. He does this by tossing out a ping pong ball five times. Those who catch the ping pong ball are selected to name, in turn, a color, a number, a city, a boy's name, and a girl's name. As each item is named, the magician writes it down on a piece of posterboard so it is large enough for the audience to read.

When all five items have been written down, the magician calls attention to an envelope threaded on a piece of crepe paper above the stage that has been suspended there throughout the performance. He climbs up on a chair, cuts the envelope down, and hands it to a volunteer. The volunteer opens the sealed envelope and inside finds a card on which the magician had correctly predicted, before the performance, all five items named by various members of the audience a few minutes ago.

This trick has two drawbacks—an assistant is necessary, and it is better performed on a stage than in a living room. But the effect is always strong, no matter where it is performed.

EQUIPMENT

Obtain a large sheet of white posterboard and a felt-tip pen, along with a stand, such as an artist's easel, for the posterboard. On this you will write the items named by the audience. You also need a long piece of crepe paper and an envelope. The envelope is threaded onto the crepe paper, which is stretched above the stage as shown in FIGURE 20.

A second envelope, identical to the one threaded on the crepe paper, and a short piece of identical crepe paper are required. This envelope should be prepared, like the other one, with slits through which the short piece of identical crepe paper is threaded as shown in FIGURE 21.

You will need a solid-backed chair (a metal folding chair will do), on the back of which you need to rig a shelf or pouch (it can be taped to the chair) as shown in FIGURE 22.

You will also need an assistant who stands offstage during the performance of the trick. The assistant has the "gimmicked" envelope and the chair with the attached pouch offstage. The assistant also has a 3-by-5 card on which he or she has written:

> The color named has to be
> Why did you think of number   ?

Fig. 20

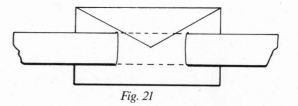

Fig. 21

One of my favorite cities is
One of my best friends is named
If I had a daughter I would name her
(your name)

You will also need a scissors and a ping pong ball.

WORKING

Before the performance, stretch the long piece of crepe paper across the front of the stage after threading the empty sealed envelope onto it.

The crepe paper can be pinned to the tops of the curtains at each side of the stage. The envelope should hang near the center and about 1 or 2 feet higher than you can reach while standing on the floor.

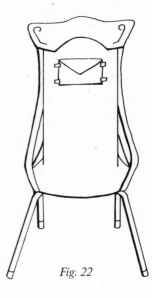

Fig. 22

Offstage your assistant has the other envelope, unsealed but threaded onto the short piece of crepe paper. The assistant also has the 3-by-5 card prepared as described above. It is important that the words already written on the 3-by-5 card be in the assistant's handwriting.

On your table are the large sheet of posterboard, the felt-tip pen, the scissors, and the ping pong ball.

Explain to the audience that you want to select five people completely at random, and that to do so you will toss out a ping pong ball five times. Whoever catches it will be selected.

Warning: Don't use this method if the audience is composed of children; they will create pandemonium scrambling and fighting for the ball. Instead, ask an adult who is present to select five children.

Today we are going to play a magic game. I want five people in the audience to name, in turn, a color, a number, a city, a boy's name, and a girl's name—but I want to select the five people at random. To do this, I'm going to toss out this ping pong ball. Whoever catches it first will name any color that comes to mind. *(Repeat this with the number, city, boy's name and girl's name.)*

Toss out the ping pong ball and ask the first person who catches it to name a color. Repeat the color aloud and write it on the posterboard in big letters with the felt-tip pen.

 Select the other four persons in the same way and have each in turn name a number, a city, a boy's name, and a girl's name. Write each of these items down in order on the cardboard.

Meanwhile, your assistant offstage hears the items named and carefully fills in the information on the 3-by-5 card.

 As soon as the fifth item is named, the assistant writes it down in the appropriate

place on the 3-by-5 card, puts the card in
the envelope, seals the envelope, and drops
it into the pouch on the back of the chair.

At this point you mention that an envelope
has been hanging above the stage since before
the performance began. You say it is time
to explain why the envelope is there.

   You pick up your scissors and try to cut
the envelope down. You can't quite reach it.
You call offstage, asking whether a ladder
is available.

It is important that you ask for a ladder
rather than a chair, for this bit of misdirection
indicates that anything that will get you up
a little higher to reach the envelope will do.

In a moment, your assistant brings forth the
chair with the pouch to the rear, unseen by
the audience. You stand up on the chair
and cut the crepe paper a few inches to the
right and left of the envelope. The loose ends
hang out of each side of the envelope.

   You should make it a point to cut the crepe
paper about the same length as that threaded
through the gimmicked envelope.

Now comes the only bit of sleight of hand
involved in the entire trick, and it is very
natural and simple. With the scissors in your

**Now, perhaps you've been wondering
about the envelope hanging here on the
stage. I think it's time to take it down and
see what's in it.**

Could I have a stepladder, please?

left hand and the envelope you've just cut
down in your right hand, start to get down
from the chair. As you do so, place your
right hand on the back of the chair to steady
yourself.

Your hand, containing the envelope, is out
of the audience's view for a split second.
That's all it takes to drop the envelope you've
just cut down into the pouch and pick up the
one your assistant has left there—the one
containing all the correct answers.

Having switched envelopes, walk to the front
of the stage, holding the new envelope with
the short piece of crepe paper threaded
through it. It appears as though the envelope
has never been out of sight of the audience.

Your assistant folds up the chair and takes
it offstage. You call a volunteer, to whom
you give the envelope. (Select the volunteer
by tossing out the ping pong ball again.)

The volunteer unseals it and reads your
predictions to the audience.

**Now, would someone in the audience
come up and open this envelope? Whoever catches this ping pong ball.**

**Now would you open the sealed enve-
lope and tell us what's inside? A 3-by-5
card? Yes, and what's written on it?
Would you read it out in a loud voice so
everyone can hear you?**

You have correctly predicted—before the performance began—the five items named by five people in the audience selected completely at random.

Thank you very much for helping me make some predictions come true.

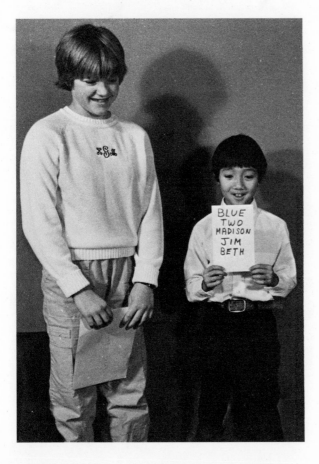

Boxing a Ring 9

EFFECT

The magician borrows a ring from someone in the audience and places it under a scarf. He attempts to make the ring disappear from under the scarf and go into the pocket of its owner. The trick seems to misfire because the ring disappears but is nowhere to be found.

The magician offers to give the owner a gift in a box as a consolation for the lost ring. The box is locked. When it is unlocked, another locked box is found inside. Inside this box is another locked box, and inside that one is still another one. There are five locked boxes in all. Inside the smallest is the borrowed ring.

EQUIPMENT

You will need a large scarf with a wide hem, with a cheap finger ring sewn into one corner of the hem. See FIGURE 23.

You will also need five boxes made of plywood, each painted a different color and fitted with a hasp for a padlock; five padlocks for the boxes; and five keys, each with a ribbon the same color as the box it opens.

The colors and sizes of the boxes are as follows: a red box 10 inches on a side, a yellow box 8 inches on a side, a green box 6 inches on a side, an orange box 4 inches on a side, and a blue box 2 inches on a side. All the boxes have hinged tops and are normal except for the second smallest box (the 4-inch one). This one is normal except that it has no bottom. See FIGURE 24.

WORKING

To set up this illusion, lock the orange box and place it inside the green box; lock the green box and place it inside the yellow box; lock the yellow box and place it inside the red box; then lock the red box.

Leave the smallest box—the blue one—unlocked and place it immediately behind the red box with the others locked inside.

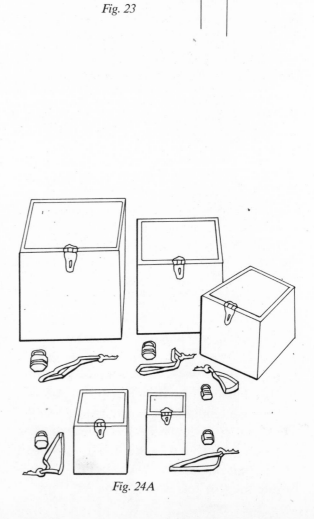

Fig. 23

Fig. 24A

Open the top of the little blue box slightly
and see that its lock is nearby. Place some
cotton in the bottom of the little blue box.

Drape the prepared scarf over the blue box
and lay your magic wand on the table near the
scarf and the blue box. See that the padlock
keys for each box with the colored ribbons
on them are nearby on your table.

Borrow a ring from someone in the audience
and call for a volunteer to hold the ring under
the scarf.

A volunteer comes up. Place the ring under
the scarf, slowly, and as you do so, grasp it in
the palm of your hand. With your thumb and
forefinger take the sewn-in ring and push
it up to the center of the scarf. Give this to
the volunteer to hold.

With the borrowed ring in your hand, walk
back to your table and pick up your magic
wand from behind the boxes. As you do this,
drop the borrowed ring in the little blue box,
close the lid, and lock it with the padlock.
The cotton in the bottom of the box prevents
the ring from making any noise as it drops in.

PATTER

Next, I'd like to borrow two things—a valuable ring and a not-so-valuable volunteer. I can promise the ring will be returned. I'm not so sure about the volunteer.

I'm going to place the ring under this scarf and get you to hold it for me. There; hold it tight, right in front of you, so everyone can see it.

Now, with the help of my magic wand I'm going to make the ring leave the scarf and magically return to its owner.

Carrying the wand, walk back to the volunteer, who is holding the ring under the scarf.

Tell the volunteer you are going to make the ring vanish from under the scarf and return to its owner in the audience.

All right, have you got a good, tight grip on the ring? Can you feel it pulling out of your fingers? It's trying to get away from you. First I'll wave my magic wand over it, then presto . . . it's gone.

Whisk the scarf from his or her hand and reveal that the ring has disappeared. Hold it out and show both sides to the audience.

The ring has vanished from your hand.

Then ask the owner of the ring to locate the ring in his or her pocket or purse. The owner checks but finds no ring there.

Now, if you'll check your pockets carefully, I think you'll find your ring has returned to you. It's not there? Oh, it must be. Did you check your wallet (*purse*)? Maybe it's hiding from you.

It looks as if something's gone wrong. Maybe the ring went to the wrong pocket.

You appeal to the volunteer on stage to check his or her pockets.

Maybe the ring went into your pocket. Will you look?

The volunteer checks his or her pockets, but of course finds no ring.

Acting embarrassed, explain that you don't know what's happened.

Offer the owner a present, whatever is in the red box, as a consolation for losing the ring.

Unlock the red box and take out the locked yellow box, placing this on top of the red box.

Unlock the yellow box and take out the green box, placing this on top of the yellow box.

Unlock the green box and take out the orange box (the one without a bottom).

By this time, the stack of boxes is rather high, so instead of putting the orange box on top of the green box, start a new stack of boxes just to the right of the others.

In doing so, bring the orange box down behind the stack of boxes (it should only be out of sight for an instant), placing it over the little blue box, and sliding the orange box to the right so the audience can see it. The little blue box, now inside the orange box, naturally slides with it.

Unlock the orange box, take out the blue box, close the cover as you've done with the others, and set the blue box on top of it.

Oh-oh. I blew it this time. I've never had this happen before. I hope you had insurance for that ring. Was it very valuable? Gee, I'm sorry about losing it. I'll tell you what I'll do, though.

I have a very valuable object in this box, and I'll give it to you to compensate for losing your ring.

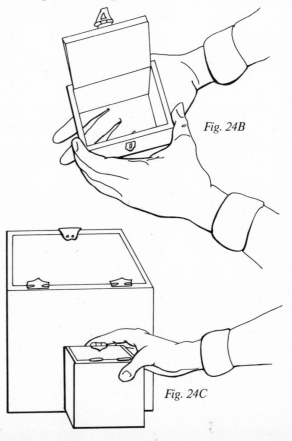

Fig. 24B

Fig. 24C

Then pick up the blue box and walk over to the volunteer with it, handing him or her both the blue box and the key with the blue ribbon on it. Ask him or her to open the blue box and to tell what he or she finds inside.

Inside is the missing ring. Ask him or her to return it to the owner.

All right, now, would you please open this box and tell everyone loudly and clearly what you find inside?

Would you take that ring to its owner, please? Is that the same ring you let me borrow? I promised I would return it to you. I guess I'll return my helper, too—in making this trick work, he (*she*) proved that he's (*she's*) valuable, too!

And, So, Good-Bye 10

EFFECT

At the conclusion of his act, the magician picks up the black table-cloth from his table and shows both sides of it. Explaining that he will do some magic sewing for his final illusion, he places in the center of the tablecloth some orange ribbon, a big sewing needle, and some thread. He folds the tablecloth once to form a sort of bag for the ribbon, needle, and thread, leaving the ends of the ribbon hanging out both ends of the baglike cloth.

When he drops the front of the cloth down so that the entire table-cloth can be seen, he reveals that the needle has magically sewn the ribbon onto the cloth, spelling out the phrase "And So Good-Bye."

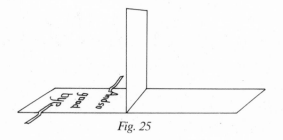

Fig. 25

Fig. 26

EQUIPMENT

The secret of this trick is in the construction of the tablecloth, which is made of heavy black cloth approximately 30 inches square. The cloth has an extra flap, exactly half the size of the full tablecloth. The flap is sewn to the center of the tablecloth as shown in FIGURE 25.

When the flap is put one way, the tablecloth appears to be black. When the flap is put the other way, the message can be seen. Put the message on the tablecloth ahead of time, using orange ribbon about ½ inch wide. First write the phrase "And So Good-Bye" on the cloth with a piece of tailor's chalk; then go back and glue the ribbon on. Use FIGURE 26 as a guide. Be sure to leave extra ribbon at the beginning and end of the "writing".

The other equipment you need is an identical orange ribbon about 20 feet long, a spool of thread, and a big sewing needle.

WORKING

Position the flap so that you will be able to show that the tablecloth is black on both sides, and put the tablecloth on the table before the performance.

Keep the thread, ribbon, and needle nearby. At the end of your show, make sure that no equipment remains on the table except the cloth.

Tell the audience you want to show them how to sew by magic and will use your tablecloth to do so, since it is the only object left on your table.

Lift up the tablecloth, carefully holding the flap in position to conceal the writing, and show both sides. Lay it on the table again and, in its center, place the ribbon, thread, and needle. Fold the cloth in half.

Now reach into the folds and pull out the two ends of the ribbon. Actually, you reach into the other side of the flap and pull out the two ends of the ribbon that are glued to the cloth—that is, the extra ribbon at the beginning of the word *And*, and the extra ribbon at the end of the word *Bye*. Lift up the cloth, which is still folded in half.

Ask the audience to chant in unison with you to make the magic work.

PATTER

And now, ladies and gentlemen, for my final demonstration, I'd like to show you how to sew—not in the regular way, but by magic. I have some ribbon, a needle, and a spool of thread. I'm going to sew the ribbon to the tablecloth—by magic.

I'll need your help to make the magic work. I'm going to command the needle by magic to sew and sew and sew and sew and sew. I'd like for you to join me in

The audience chants in unison with you. Just when they have finished, and have said "sew" for the fifth time, drop down the front half of the cloth, but hold on to the flap and the rest of the cloth at the top. There is the ribbon, magically sewn onto the cloth and spelling out, "And So Good-Bye."

unison, saying, "Sew and sew and sew and sew and sew," exactly five times.

All right. Let's begin now, all together. Needle, I want you to sew and sew and sew and sew and sew.

And so good-bye.

Presentation, Patter, and 11
Miscellaneous Tidbits

The word *presentation* is used to describe how a trick is performed for an audience; that is, what the magician says and does—how he introduces and presents an illusion. The importance of the presentation of magic cannot be stressed too much. Almost anyone can learn to do a trick that will fool an audience. But this is not enough. The illusion must be presented to the audience in a way that is not only baffling but also entertaining. In fact, some say that conjuring is 10 percent skill and 90 percent showmanship. A simple trick that draws "ho hums" from an audience in the hands of an amateur can seem the most baffling illusion in the hands of a professional magician skilled in the art of presentation.

The entire presentation of a trick depends greatly on the specific personality of the performer, but there are dozens of audience-tested jokes, flourishes, and bits of humor that will aid any beginner in presenting illusions in an entertaining manner.

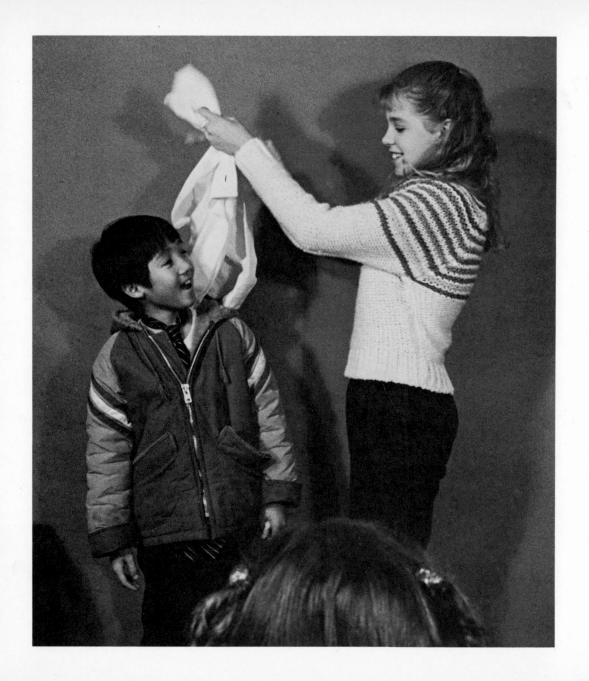

This chapter lists and describes briefly some of the many ideas developed by magicians over the years. Some may seem "corny" in print, but they never fail to entertain a live audience. Try them. Most of the ideas listed here are designed to be worked into your act wherever they seem appropriate.

Nothing up My Sleeves: This is an extremely effective and amusing opener for your show. Cut the sleeves from an old long-sleeved shirt, and just before you begin your show, slide them on your arms over your regular shirt or blouse. Then put on a suit jacket or sweater and walk out before the audience.

Say, "Every time I do a magic show there's at least one person in the audience that pops up and says, 'I know how he does it. He's got something up his jacket (or sweater) sleeves.' I want to assure you that I have nothing up my jacket (sweater) sleeves. . . . Nothing, that is, but my shirt sleeves. And if it'll make you feel any better, I'll get rid of them."

With that remark, unbutton the fake shirt sleeves and pull them out of your jacket or sweater sleeves and off your arms, and toss them aside. Then go on to your first illusion.

Shirt off the Back: Arrange ahead of time for one of the men present to assist you, preferably someone wearing a jacket and a necktie. Have him take his shirt off and put it back on like a cape, draped over his back. He should button the top two or three buttons of his shirt and put his tie back on. Then he should bring the sleeves alongside his arms and button the sleeve buttons around his wrists. Then, when he puts the coat back on, it appears as if he were wearing his shirt normally.

At the end of your act, say that you think it's time for one of the adults to come up and assist you with your final trick, since it is a very dangerous one. Get the man with the gimmicked shirt to come up and have a seat on stage, facing the audience. Go to your table behind him and pick up a handsaw. You can joke about how you are going to try the "sawing the man in half" trick. Discard this idea after feeling the man's stomach, saying he is too tough and might break your saw.

Then tell the audience that you will try to cut him in half another way. Remark that the man seems to be worried and is getting a little hot under the collar. Walk over to him and unbutton the two or three buttons at the top of his shirt and fan him a little with your hand. Unbutton the cuff buttons, too. Then grasp the collar of the man's shirt and pull it straight up. The shirt will come right out from under his coat and right off his back, leaving him sitting there with his coat and tie on but without his shirt. Hand him his shirt and thank him for helping you.

Irribatti Wambadoo: An effective routine is to tell the audience that every magician has a magic word or words that he calls on from time to time to help him accomplish his magic. Tell them that you have a magic word, too, and pronounce it for them. The funnier-sounding nonsense word you pick, the better. I use the words *irribatti wambadoo,* for instance. Just the strange sound of such a word usually gets a laugh.

Tell the audience members they'll have to help you with the magic by saying the magic word. Then tell them you will test it first. Explain that you would like them all to say the magic words, *irribatti wambadoo,* together, at the count of three. You count to three and they all say it together. You look very disappointed and say, "That certainly won't make any magic happen; it wasn't loud enough. Let's try it again, louder this time."

The second time you do it, they yell so loudly that the rafters almost shake. But you look disappointed again. You say, "That was a little better but still not loud enough to make magic really work. Let's try it again, and this time let's really make it loud."

When you do it the third time, the yell will be so loud that the rafters really will shake. You look pleased and say, "That's more like it. I think that'll really make my magic work." Several times later in the show, you might want to count to three and have the audience yell the magic word. This not only gives them a sense of participation in the show but it also gives younger children a chance to work off excess energy.

Music: Many amateur magicians as well as professional conjurors find that a musical interlude heightens the audience's interest in a magic show. Music should be used especially with illusions that are self-explanatory and visible, not requiring patter. Perhaps the easiest way for a part-time magician to manage such music is with a small cassette player. You can prerecord the music you want on a blank cassette and keep that cassette with your other magical props.

You might go through your record collection and record instrumental music that would be appropriate for certain tricks. During your performance the cassette player can be kept at the rear of your table and turned on and off with the flick of a switch. Thus there is no need for an offstage assistant to handle your music.

Explaining a Trick: If you have a cassette player and use music with some effects, you might want to try the following as a laugh-getter. At a certain place on the cassette, have music playing very low. When you have just finished performing a baffling illusion, tell the audience that you are now going to explain just how you did it. As you say this, the music plays softly.

Then start to explain how the trick was done. At this point the music begins to get louder and louder (you have recorded it this way ahead of time). Finally the music is so loud that you cannot be heard above it, and the audience sees you standing there talking and gesturing as you "explain" to them how you did the trick. But of course they cannot hear a word you are saying. This situation continues for about half a minute.

Then the music begins to get soft again, and you can make yourself heard above it. At this point you have finished "explaining" how the trick was done. Just as the music gets soft enough for the audience once again to hear you, say, ". . . and there, ladies and gentlemen, is the complete explanation of how that illusion was accomplished. You can do it yourself when you get home tonight."

Card File: As you perform more magic shows and add more tricks to your repertoire, you will find it handy to keep a file of the illusions you perform. A simple and convenient way to do this is to use 3-by-5 cards. You will find it much simpler when planning a show simply to look through your cards than to rummage through your props.

A simple way to keep these records is as follows: List the name of an effect at the top of each card. Next, include a brief paragraph under the heading of "Preparation." Here list the props you need and where they should be when the show starts. Next, include a paragraph under the heading "Patter." Write very briefly the story line or the key phrases of the patter you will use.

You will find these cards extremely useful, not only in lining up the effects for a particular show, but also in reviewing just before a performance to make sure you have all the necessary props, have them in the right place, and have your patter line firmly in mind.

I have also found it handy to keep a record, on 3-by-5 cards, of magic shows I have performed. This, too, is a simple operation. At the top of each card simply list the date, time, and place of the show, along with the approximate number of people who attended and what organization they were from. Next list the tricks performed.

You will find such records handy after you've done a number of shows, particularly if you're called for a repeat performance. Knowing precisely the illusions you previously performed for a particular group will allow you to work up a new show when called to perform for the same group.

Fig. 27

Applause Card: You'll need an easily made prop for this laugh-getter. Construct a card in the following manner: Cut one piece of white cardboard to the size of 10 by 14 inches. On one side of this card attach a flap horizontally, hinged at the center. The flap should be 5 by 14 inches. Thus the flap can be flipped up or down to reveal two separate messages on one side of the card.

Next, on the side of the card without the flap, print the words "THANK YOU." On the side with the flap, print two messages, one that will show when the flap is up, and another that will show when the flap is down. The two messages are: "APPLAUSE PLEASE" and "BOTH OF YOU." See FIGURE 27.

To get ready to use this prop, put the flap up so that the words "APPLAUSE PLEASE" show. When you finish an illusion, pick up the card from the table and hold it so the audience can see it. When they read the words "APPLAUSE PLEASE," they will applaud.

When the applause subsides, turn the card over so they can read the words "THANK YOU." The flap side of the card is now toward you. Simply flip down the flap, revealing the words "BOTH OF YOU." Now turn the card around and show it to the audience.

Patter Gag Lines: Most libraries have books on humor that contain short gags. One good way to liven up your magic act and add humor to your program is to search through these books for one-liners that will fit in with your particular program. Try to find gags that match your personality and fall naturally into your act.

A good way to select gags is by association. If you do a rope trick, for example, find short jokes about ropes. With practice you will find that when you pick up your piece of rope to do your trick, the rope itself will remind you of several rope gags. Through association, the gags become an important part of the trick.

While the types of gags are unlimited, here are a few short ones that could fit in with almost any program:

• When you first walk on stage at the beginning of a show: "Good evening, ladies and gentlemen. My name is (*state your name*) and I want you to know I'm the greatest magician in the world . . . by that name."

• Right after you've introduced yourself to the audience: "I'm going to try to deceive you a little and entertain you a lot this evening. I'd like everybody to sit back and relax while we take off on a magic carpet ride. (*Stop; stare at the back row.*) I see some people in the back row who really took me seriously. They've gone to sleep!

"Speaking of going to sleep . . . when I sleep I have a bad habit. I snore very loudly. I used to snore so loudly that I woke myself up. But I solved that problem. Now I sleep in the next room."

• When the audience applauds: "I really appreciate that applause. You're a very enthusiastic audience. They're not all that way. Last week I did a show for the most unenthusiastic audience I've ever seen. During the whole evening I got only one "applau". That group made about as much noise as a caterpillar walking across a Persian carpet . . . with tennis shoes on!"

• When you finish a trick and the audience doesn't applaud: "That's strange; the instructions that came with this trick said it was a baffling and entertaining mystery. Actually, it's really not much of a trick, but I paid a lot of money for it."

• When starting to perform a trick: "This next effect won first prize at the annual magicians' convention. They didn't actually give me the silver loving cup. But they did give me the little rubber mat it sat on."

• Just after finishing a trick: "You know, I also do mind reading. I have a fantastic memory. There are only three things I ever forget. I can't remember names. And I can't remember phone numbers. And the third thing? Now, what was the third thing? Sorry. I can't remember."

• If you happen to make an obvious mistake while performing a trick: "What can you expect of a day that starts with getting up in the morning?"

• At any time during your performance, look at someone in the audience and say: "Is your seat comfortable? Can you see all right? Do you feel a draft? No? Let's you and me change places."

• Just as you start to do a card trick: "I do a few tricks, but I only play one card game. That's solitaire. I should give it up, though, because I cheat all the time. But I've never caught myself cheating. I'm too clever for that."

• Just before doing the last trick in your program: "And now for the final illusion of the evening. You know, my magic shows always have a happy ending. People are always happy to see them end."

A Ten-Minute 12
Magic Show without Props

Once you've given a few magic shows and established your reputation as a magician, there invariably will be occasions when you will be called on to perform at small social gatherings. There you are, completely unprepared and without a single magical prop! What do you do? Beg off, saying you're not prepared? Of course not. You perform without props or preparation.

This chapter contains several illusions which can be performed anywhere, any time, and without advance preparation. There's enough here for a 10-minute show. Perform these tricks only, leaving your audience wanting more, and tell them where and when they can catch your next stage performance.

A Prediction

EFFECT

You write a number on a slip of paper, fold the paper, and give it to someone to hold. Then you direct someone else in the audience to select any three-digit number and reverse the order of digits in that number. Then have that person subtract the smaller number from the larger one, and reverse the order of digits in the answer. Have that person add the answer and the "reversed" answer. He or she reaches the final sum, finding you had predicted it accurately even before the selection of the original number.

EQUIPMENT

A slip of paper and a pencil

WORKING

Write on a slip of paper the number 1,089, fold the paper, and give it to someone in the audience to hold. No one but you knows what you've written on the paper.

Ask another person in the audience to select any three-digit number as long as the three digits are all different.

PATTER

I'm going to write a number down on this paper. Would you hold on to it for me, please? Thank you.

Now I'll need another volunteer. All right, would you please select a three-digit number? It can be any three-digit number, as long as the digits are all different.

The calculation proceeds as follows (in this example, 741 is the number originally selected):

$$741$$
$$-147$$
$$594$$

$$594$$
$$+495$$
$$1{,}089$$

If you follow this procedure, the answer will always be 1,089 and you can always predict it correctly. Be sure to tell the person that when he or she makes the first subtraction the answer should be a *three*-digit result even if it means placing a zero at the far left.

An added touch is to show the answer upside down (after the person has done the arithmetic). When 1,089 is upside down it looks like 6,801. When it appears that you have predicted incorrectly, simply say, "Sorry, I'm holding it upside down," and turn the paper right side up, showing 1,089.

Obviously, this effect can be done only once for an audience. It can be developed into a larger stage effect by using a blackboard so that the whole audience can see the numbers.

Would you please reverse the digits of that number and subtract the smaller three-digit number from the larger one?

All right, now please reverse the digits of *that* three-digit number. Add the number and the reversed number together.

Reading Your Thoughts

EFFECT

You draw a small (about ¾-inch) Greek letter omega (see FIGURE 28) in the center of a slip of paper from a small pad, about 2½ by 3½ inches. You hand the slip of paper to someone in the audience and ask him or her to write a number, a color, a short phrase—anything he or she would like—within the omega. You ask the person to fold the paper twice and give it back to you. When he or she does, you tear the paper into small pieces, put them in an ashtray, and set fire to them. (Be sure to keep the fire small and confined!)

You ask the person who wrote the message to stare into the flames and concentrate on what he wrote. As the flames turn the last bits of paper to ashes, you state correctly what was written on the paper unseen by you.

EQUIPMENT

A small pad of paper, a pencil, and matches

WORKING

This trick is accomplished by what is known as the *centerfold tear.* You control the position of the message by telling the volunteer to write within the omega.

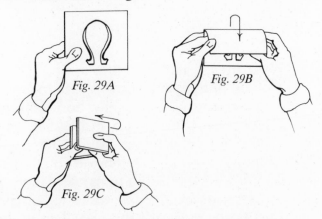

Fig. 29A

Fig. 29B

Fig. 29C

Folding the paper twice (see FIGURE 29) brings the message to the upper right-hand corner of the folded paper. Take the folded paper from the volunteer without really looking at it. *Immediately* begin tearing it to bits.

When it is in small pieces, slide the center portion—the piece at the upper right-hand corner—into your right hand and drop the remaining pieces into an ashtray.

PATTER

Fig. 28

I'd like to present an experiment in mind reading. On this slip of paper I'll draw the Greek letter omega. As you may know, mystery has always been associated with that letter. I'd like to ask someone with strong powers of concentration to write something within this omega. It can be anything that comes to mind: your telephone number, a color, a name, a short phrase, a foreign word, anything. Would you go ahead and write it inside the omega, please? Thank you.

After you've written it, please fold the paper in half. Now fold it again. Now hand me the paper, please.

If you'd feel more comfortable getting rid of the center portion at this point, simply reach into the right pocket of your sweater, pants, or skirt, leave the center portion there, bring out a book of matches, and hand it to the person who is going to light the slips of paper.

You can retrieve the center portion by reaching into your pocket to get the pad of paper to write on. This is not necessary, however, because no one suspects you have anything in your hand at this point.

Ask the person who did the writing to light the pieces of paper with a match.

As the paper is burning and all attention is focused on the flames, unfold the center portion of the paper with your pencil point as it rests on top of the pad of paper. Read the message. Now you're ready to "read the thoughts" of your volunteer.

How do you do this without being discovered by the audience? Simply pick up the pad of paper in your right hand (along with the folded middle section of the torn-up paper) and pretend to write something on the pad.

Pretend to make a mistake and rip off that sheet, crumple it up, and stuff it in your pocket. The center section goes with it.

Now, please light the bits of paper I've torn up and, as they burn, stare into the flames. At the same time, concentrate on what you wrote on the paper. Put everything else out of your mind; concentrate only on the message you wrote, which is now burning to ashes. I'll have to ask everyone in the room to remain absolutely quiet for the next minute or so. It's impossible to receive thought waves if there is the slightest bit of noise.

You are now free to write the volunteer's thoughts (which you have by now read from the folded middle section of the torn-up paper) on the new top sheet of the pad.

At this point, it is best to drag the trick out a bit, doing a bit of acting. Assume, for example, the person wrote the words *good show.*

Write the message down and hand it to the person who originally wrote the message inside the omega, reading what you have written. It is the same; you have successfully read his or her mind.

Your thoughts are beginning to come through to me now. The message is rather hazy but it seems to be getting clearer. I'm sure you didn't write a number. It was a word. No, it was more than one word. I think it was two words . . . and they both seem to be short words. In fact, I see two words, each a short word and each with the same number of letters . . . four letters each, I think. There appear to be round letters in the words; there must be several *o*'s. Yes, now it's becoming clearer. The first word is *good*. And the second word? Could it be *ship*? No, not *ship. Show.* That's it. *Good show.* Is that what you wrote? *Good show*?

EFFECT

You ask someone to write on a piece of paper the numbers one through nine, with the exception of eight. Then you ask that person to look over those digits and tell you which one is written in the poorest handwriting. Which one does the writer need to practice?

When he or she tells you, you give him or her a two-digit number and tell him or her to multiply the eight-digit number by it. The answer turns out to be a long string of numbers all the same. The repeated number is the one he or she needed practice in writing.

Poor Handwriting

EQUIPMENT

A piece of paper and a pencil

WORKING

PATTER

I'd like to give someone with poor handwriting a chance to practice and improve his (*her*) handwriting. Who would like to volunteer? Good. Please write across the top of this paper the number 12345679. That's right, skip the 8.

Now, will you look at each of the digits you wrote and tell me which one is written in the poorest handwriting? In other words, of all those digits, which one would you say you most needed to practice writing? The 6? All right.

To achieve the effect, simply multiply in your head the number the volunteer says he or she needs practice in writing by the number 9. Tell him or her to multiply the long string of numbers by that number.

For example, if the volunteer says he or she needs practice in writing 5, tell him or her to multiply the long number (12345679) by 45 (9 times 5). If the volunteer needs practice in writing 7, tell him or her to multiply by 63 (9 times 7). If the volunteer

says 3, tell him or her to multiply by 27
(9 times 3). And so on.

**I'm going to ask you to do one thing.
Please multiply the entire number —
12345679 — by 54.**

This is what happens:

$$
\begin{array}{r}
12345679 \\
\times 54 \\
\hline
49382716 \\
61728395 \\
\hline
666666666
\end{array}
$$

**There; you've gotten a little practice in
writing 6 — the number you said you most
needed to practice.**

EFFECT

You ask a person in the audience to think of any word, phrase, number, or old saying, in any language or dialect. Once the person has it firmly in mind, he or she should concentrate on it alone and put all other thoughts out of his or her mind. You concentrate on reading his or her thoughts and finally write something on a slip of paper. Then you fold the paper and hand it to someone else in the audience —someone across the room.

Now you tell the person whose mind you were reading to announce to everyone in the room what it was he or she was thinking. He or she does this. You tell the person holding the paper on which you wrote your prediction to unfold it and read aloud what you had written there. It turns out to be exactly the same.

A Miracle Prediction

EQUIPMENT

A piece of paper and a pencil

WORKING	PATTER
	Now I'd like to try an experiment in pure and simple mind reading. I want someone in the audience to volunteer to allow me to try to read his thoughts. You—will you please think of a word or a phrase or a line from a poem—anything that comes to mind. I don't care how short or long it is; in fact I don't care whether it is in English or another language. Make it as difficult for me as you can.
Choose a volunteer and have him or her think of a word or phrase.	
	Take your time to think of something. Change your mind as often as you like. Just let me know when you've finally settled on something. Okay? Do you have it in mind now?
While the volunteer is concentrating on the word or phrase he or she has mentally selected, ham it up as though you were having an extremely difficult time reading his or her thoughts.	**All right, please put all other thoughts out of your mind and concentrate on that one thing alone—nothing else. Please, I'll have to ask for absolute silence while I'm trying to receive these thought waves.**
Now begin acting. Go through all sorts of mental anguish trying to receive the thought	**I'm sorry; your thoughts are not coming to me clearly. Please, if you're thinking**

waves. Close your eyes. Wrinkle your brow. Look puzzled.

Suddenly, look relieved, and write on the paper, "Exactly the same." Fold it up and give it to someone across the room.

Then ask the volunteer to announce aloud what he or she was concentrating on.

When the volunteer does this, ask the person across the room to open the paper and read what you wrote.

He or she reads off: "Exactly the same." The audience is flabbergasted. If others want to verify what you've written, let them look. Then they too are in on the secret.

But many people in the room—especially if you're doing this in a large hall—will not get a chance to look at the paper. For those who do, they've witnessed a good gag. For those who don't, they've seen a miracle they'll be telling people about for the next month.

of two things at once, put one of them out of your mind. Concentrate only on the one thing you decided to transmit to me by thought waves.

I'm not sure, but I did get a clear flash of thought, just for an instant, and then it faded away. But I think I got it. You—will you hold this piece of paper on which I've made a prediction?

And you, will you tell everyone here just what it was you were thinking of?

And now, would you unfold the paper you're holding and read to the audience what I've written there?

EFFECT

You make a prediction and write it on a slip of paper without showing it to the audience. You fold the paper and let someone in the audience hold it until later.

Then you write a four-digit number on another sheet of paper and invite a member of the audience to write any four-digit number that comes to mind under the number you wrote. You write another four-digit number under that one and invite another member of the audience to write any four-digit number that comes to mind under it. Then you write still another four-digit number under that one.

When the column of figures is added up, the total is found to be the exact total you had predicted ahead of time.

EQUIPMENT

Some paper and a pencil

Predicting a Number

WORKING

The number you predict should be between 21,000 and 29,000. For example, assume the number you predict is 24, 286. Write this down on a slip of paper but do not show it to anyone. Fold the paper and give it to someone in the audience to hold.

Then write the first four-digit number on another piece of paper and show this to the audience.

The point to remember is that the first four-digit number you write down should be the number you have predicted minus 20,000, plus 2.

For example, if you have predicted 24, 286, drop 20,000, making the four-digit number 4,286, and then add 2, making 4,288. Now write down 4,288.

PATTER

I had a very strange arithmetic teacher when I was in school. Most of the teachers taught us to put down the sums, add them up, and arrive at an answer. But this teacher was different. She taught us to write down the answer first and then put down the sums. Did you ever hear of teaching arithmetic like that?

I'll show you. First, I'll write down the answer on this slip of paper. I'll show it to you later, not right now.

Will you guard the answer carefully?

Now let's work on the sums. I'm going to write down a four-digit number; for example, 4,288.

Have someone in the audience write down a four-digit number. Whatever he or she writes, you then write under that a four-digit number that would make 9,999 if the number were added to yours.

For example, if he or she writes a 6, you'll write a 3 under it; if he or she writes a 4, you'll write a 5 under it.

Have someone else in the audience write down a four-digit number. Again, write under it a four-digit number that would make 9,999. Now there should be five four-digit numbers.

Here is how the effect works:

Your prediction unseen by the audience	24,286
Therefore your first four-digit number is	4,288
The first member of the audience writes	6,793
Therefore you write	3,206
The second member of the audience writes	8,527
Therefore you write	1,472
The total	24,286 (your prediction)

Now, please write a four-digit number right under that one. Anything that comes to mind. Don't allow me to influence you. Just write any four-digit number that pops into your head.

Now, let's get someone else in on the act. How about you; will you write any four-digit number that comes to mind right under the number I've written?

Have the second volunteer add the five numbers and compare the total with the number you wrote down on the folded slip of paper earlier.

Now, you seem to be good at arithmetic. Will you please total these numbers? What's that, the total is 24,286? If you'll take a look at the folded slip of paper on which I wrote a number before we began this experiment, you'll see that I wrote down the total before we even began with our sums!

EFFECT

You place a 50-cent piece in the palm of your hand and cover it with a handkerchief. You invite several people in the room to feel under the handkerchief to make sure the coin is still there. Then you whisk away the handkerchief and reveal that the coin has vanished. It mysteriously returns in the same way.

EQUIPMENT

A 50-cent piece and a handkerchief

The Disappearing Coin

WORKING

This trick is accomplished with the help of a confederate in the audience.

Place the coin in your upturned palm and cover it with a handkerchief.

Invite several people to make sure the coin is still there.

The last person you ask to feel the coin is your confederate. He or she feels the coin and, unknown to the others in the audience, takes it away in his or her hand.

You then whisk away the handkerchief and show that the coin has vanished.

To make the coin come back, simply reverse the procedure. Several people feel under the handkerchief to make sure the coin has not returned.

The last one is your confederate, who places the coin back on your palm. You then pull away the handkerchief and show that the coin has mysteriously returned.

PATTER

Money gets away from us pretty fast these days. I can illustrate how fast with this 50-cent piece. For example, if I put it in my hand and cover it up with a handkerchief, it should fly away.

There; will you feel under the handkerchief to make sure it's still there? Is it? Will you check and see? And you? Please feel to see if the coin is still there. You all know it's there, but is it really?

Now, let's try to make it come back.

Will you feel to see if the coin has returned? No? Will you check, please? Still not there? And you? No?

But I feel it coming back. . . .

Conclusion

These short, entertaining tricks are sure to whet your audience's appetite for the more involved effects you know. Once you've mastered all the tricks in this book, you'll want to learn more. Get as much practice as you can actually performing magic in front of other people.

But always remember to keep the key to a trick a secret. The mystery behind a magic trick is the source of enjoyment for the people watching it. If they learn how a trick has been done, it will no longer interest them.

The rewards of performing magic are many. It's possible to earn money by giving shows at gatherings, such as birthday parties. Doing tricks in front of people can help to build your confidence and make you more relaxed when you speak to groups. And it can also improve your ability to work with your hands.

Above all, though, you should perform magic because you enjoy doing so. Illusions should entertain your audiences, but, just as important, they should fascinate and intrigue you. Your enjoyment will be reflected in the quality of your performances.

About the Author

In *Illusions Illustrated,* James W. Baker has combined two of his greatest loves, writing and magic.

From 1963 until 1983, Baker was a publications specialist for the United States Information Agency, editing various Agency magazines for distribution outside the United States. During his years with the Agency, Baker and his family lived in India, Turkey, Pakistan, the Philippines, and Tunisia and traveled in more than 50 other countries. They now make their home in Williamsburg, Virginia.

A serious amateur magician for more than 25 years, Baker has performed magic shows in hospitals, orphanages, and schools throughout the world. He is a charter member of Ring 177 of the International Brotherhood of Magicians in Bangalore, India; a former member of the brotherhood's National Capital Ring 50 in Washington, D.C.; a member of the Society of American Magicians; and a past president of the Philippines Amateur League of Magicians in Manila.

$14.00

$14.00

||